PENTECOST 3

**INTERPRETING
THE LESSONS OF
THE CHURCH YEAR**

**PATRICIA
WILSON-KASTNER**

**PROCLAMATION 5
SERIES B**

FORTRESS PRESS   MINNEAPOLIS

PROCLAMATION

PROCLAMATION 5
Interpreting the Lessons of the Church Year
Series B, Pentecost 3

Cover and interior design: Spangler Design Team

Library of Congress Cataloging-in-Publication Data available

ISBN 0-8006-4192-2

The paper used in this publication meets the minimum requirements of American National Standard for Information Sciences—Permanence of Paper for Printed Library Materials, ANSI Z329.48-1984. ∞™

Manufactured in the U.S.A.   AF 1-4192

98   97   96   95   94   1   2   3   4   5   6   7   8   9   10

CONTENTS

Introduction

Pentecost 3 is the final part of the Pentecost cycle of the church year. As we in the church increasingly appreciate, the season of Pentecost is a time of reflection on the growth in the Christian life. Advent-Christmas-Epiphany and Lent-Eastertide-Pentecost developed in observance of specific festivals connected to the calendar. The time after Pentecost is the time that is *not* Advent or Eastertide or some other specific festival. In that sense, it is not an intentional season. It is "ordinary time," not celebrating any particular event or action, in its character neither penitential nor festal.

Pentecost season is ordinary in another sense. It is the time of prayer and reflection about the ordinary dimensions of the Christian life, its growth and development, its challenges and rewards in daily life. If the great seasons celebrate the hills and valleys of the Christian life, Pentecost time focuses on the trek across the plains that constitutes most of the Christian pilgrimage for the majority of people. It is the time for the continuous reading of the Synoptic Gospels' accounts of the active life and teachings of Jesus, the Old Testament relationship to his ministry, and our following of a major New Testament letter.

During this season we settle down for serious reflection about how we as a community and as individuals live the Christian life in this world with eyes that also see God's eternity amidst our time. In this volume, our particular segment of that liturgical time is the last section, Pentecost 3, the final two months of the season. In the Gospel, we finish that part of the continuous reading of Mark which precedes Jesus' triumphal entry into Jerusalem. That *lectio continua* concludes on the next to the last Sunday. For the most part, our epistle is Hebrews, while the Old Testament readings are selected from various books, with an eye to their relationship to the Gospel reading.

In any year of the liturgical cycle the last Sunday of Pentecost is always the feast of Christ the King, whether given that name in the official liturgical calendar or not. The collect and readings celebrate Jesus' sovereignty in the drama of redemption in human history. The celebration of Jesus as Lord (*kurios*) of history offers a theological perspective from which both to conclude the liturgical year and to lead the community back to its entry into a new liturgical year.

In this volume of the Proclamation series, the first part of each section is exegetical; the second specifically explores homiletical ideas. Where some of the different major lectionaries differ from the common readings, I have indicated that divergence, and focused on the Common Lectionary in the

5

explorations. Particularly in the homiletical interpretations, I have concentrated on the Common Lectionary.

I am not one of those who believes that a Sunday sermon must comment on all three of the readings. Sometimes all three readings are related, but usually the epistle has no connection to the other two, and at times the Old Testament seems quite artificially matched with the Gospel. My own approach is to assume that ordinarily in the sermon one of the readings will supply the major theme, and the other selections may complement or comment on it. I am also firmly convinced that the good news of God's love is contained throughout the entire Bible; a good gospel sermon can be preached about any of the scriptural readings.

Twentieth Sunday after Pentecost

Lutheran	Roman Catholic	Episcopal	Common Lectionary
Gen. 2:18-24	Gen. 2:18-24	Gen. 2:18-24	Gen. 2:18-24
Heb. 2:9-11, (12-18)	Heb. 2:9-11	Heb. 2:(1-8), 9-18	Heb. 1:1-4; 2:9-11
Mark 10:2-16	Mark 10:2-16 *or* 10:2-12	Mark 10:2-9	Mark 10:2-16

EXEGETICAL INTERPRETATION

First Lesson: Genesis 2:18-24. The Genesis reading has been used over the course of Biblical interpretation both to proclaim the inferiority of women and, alternately, the equality of women and men. One scholar, tongue in cheek, even suggests that the creation of woman last, after man and the animals, intimates woman's superiority.) However, the primary purpose of the section is suggested by its matching with the reading from Mark about marriage, divorce, and children. It is primarily an etiological explanation about marriage, as suggested by verse 24.

The story is generally acknowledged as part of the J, or Jahwist, tradition, deriving from an earlier set of creation stories than Gen. 1:1—2:3, the Priestly (P) account. The telling of human origins at God's hands is clearly a concrete narrative of divine action and human response in creation, in distinction from the later and more liturgically formed and hymnodic account. The P story poetically expresses a hieratic interconnection of all creation. Its story of human creation relates that God said, "let us create humankind in our image, according to our likeness; and let them have dominion over all the . . . animals."

Our J account shows us images of God's creation: divine hands scoop up the mud of the primordial garden to make Adam, the first human; Adam's dominion over creation is expressed through his naming of the creatures. The J story then answers the great mythic question humans pose: Why are humans erotically attracted to each other? Such a question is not just about sexual attraction, but about the community that is essential to humanity. It is not good to be alone. Aloneness is incomplete. The couple's need for each other is not just about sex, but about the necessary completion of solitary humanity. In the biblical vision, humans are created as social.

Ezer, the word the narrator chooses to describe the woman whom God will create, is a term commonly used for God as helper, completer of what mortals cannot do. Thus the term does not denote inferiority, or even the modern theory of complementarity. As in the first creation story, woman and man are of the same human nature. In this case, woman is created out of Adam's rib, "bone of my bone, and flesh of my flesh." The paronomasia between *ish* (man) and *ishsha* (woman) reminds the hearers of the partnership between man and woman, which before the fall is expressed in what might well be called "original equality."

The subordination of woman comes only after Adam and Eve sin. In the Garden of Eden they are equals. We even find rabbinical traditions which assert that when the Messiah comes, the condition of women will be higher than that of men, thus referring us back to the time of Eden. The original vision of marriage is therefore of the relationship of two equals, who each require the other to complete their humanity, and who voluntarily and joyfully find each other and live in faithful companionship.

The etiological motivation is clearly expressed: "*therefore* a man leaves his father and mother, and cleaves to his wife, and they become one flesh." The unity is far more than sexual, while certainly including that dimension of humanity. "Flesh" includes all of the human condition—rejoicing, mourning, loving, hating, bearing children and raising them, caring for parents, laboring in the home, tending to field and flock, as well as sexual attraction and loneliness—everything that is part of the human condition. Humans want and need to share those experiences; marriage is the central relationship of the human community through which we are all interrelated.

At creation, Adam and Eve were unself-consciously naked—without embarrassment or fear. The nakedness was an expression of frank sexuality as a normal part of the human condition; it was also a sign of their trusting and open relationship with each other, free of envy, blame, and all the evils that the fall would bring.

Second Lesson: Hebrews 2:9-11, (12-18). Selections from the Letter to the Hebrews will be used for the rest of the Sundays after Pentecost until the last Sunday, the feast of Christ the King. Thus some background on the Letter to the Hebrews seems appropriate. A letter written in elegantly crafted Greek, on literary grounds it is not by Paul's hand, and in the early church only some Alexandrians had placed it among Paul's letters. Various authors have been suggested, such as Apollos and Prisca, but Origen's judgment about authorship is the most succinct and clear: "God alone knows."

The letter seems addressed to the second generation after Christ, who have seen persecutions and distress, and need encouragement to continue a faithful life as Christians. Their Bible is the Septuagint, so it appears probable that they are converted Greek-speaking Jews. One can make a case for the date being before or after the destruction of the Jerusalem Temple in 70 C.E., because both Jewish and Christian authors continued to write about temple worship after its destruction.

The letter itself has the character of a sermon, rather than an epistle. Its primary concern is to strengthen the faith of those who are ceasing to believe in Jesus by comparing the person and work of Jesus to the worship of the Jerusalem cultus. Jesus is presented both as the human "pioneer and perfecter of our faith" and as the great High Priest, who has entered into the heavenly temple, offering the perfect sacrifice of himself on our behalf. Its primary themes are the superiority of Jesus to the angels, the prophets, and Moses himself; the superiority of Jesus' priesthood to that of the levitical priesthood; and the definitive and perfect character of his sacrifice as opposed to the limited and inadequate sacrifice of the Jerusalem cultus. The Old Testament is read typologically: the Jerusalem temple, for instance, is an inadequate rendering of the heavenly temple and altar in which Jesus makes his sacrifice.

The Common Lectionary reading is the only one to introduce this series of readings from Hebrews by using 1:1-4, which contains an elegantly stated introduction to the epistle, contrasting the various ways God has spoken to our ancestors with the finality of our redemption in Christ. God is one, and God's work is unified, but is done in differing ways. Now it is fulfilled in Jesus, whose heavenly being and earthly existence and priestly work are both referred to.

The Episcopal Lectionary allows the reading of 2:1-8, which is part of the proof of Jesus' superiority to the angels. All the lectionaries read 2:9-11; the Episcopalians and the Lutherans (for whom it is optional) continue with vv. 12-18. Clearly vv. 9-11 are the focus of the reading, which is brief, but loaded with theological significance. The introductory verses affirm the two dimensions of Christ's reality. He is God's appointed heir and the one through whom the world was created, "the reflection of God's glory and the exact imprint of God's very being," through whom all things are sustained. At the same time, Jesus is also the priest, who "has made purification for sins." For the author of Hebrews, the earthly life and work of Jesus must be seen and understood in the context of the heavenly being of Jesus.

Verse 9 of chapter 2 speaks of the now-exalted Jesus, who was for a time made lower than the angels, although by nature he is superior to them, now "crowned with glory and honor." The "glory and honor," which certainly are intended to resonate with the glory of God's presence in the temple, are linked quite directly and specifically with Jesus' suffering and

9

death, which are his priestly sacrifice on behalf of everyone. These ideas are fundamental in Hebrews: First, the exaltation of the earthly Jesus is a direct consequence of his suffering; second, his suffering and death were not just personal, but priestly, on behalf of the world.

The earthly Jesus, in verses 10-11, is praised as the pioneer, the one who goes before and makes the place—in this case, the heavenly city—ready for those who follow him. Jesus' complete humanity roots his saving work as a priest for all humanity. In this sense his priesthood is utterly inclusive; it is for all. Because he is the pioneer and priest for all children of a common father God, Jesus is brother to all. God's asking work through Jesus extends to all.

Perfection is another key notion in this epistle. Perfection is not moral betterment, but achieving its end (*telos*). One of the aspects of Jesus' perfection is that it is achieved through suffering. The suffering is his passion and crucifixion, seen as fulfilling the typology of the temple sacrifice, especially the atonement sacrifice. Much of the epistle explores Jesus' suffering in this context, and how it perfects not only Jesus, but all humanity. Verses 12-18 in the Lutheran and Episcopal lectionaries continue these themes, using Old Testament references.

Gospel: Mark 10:2-16. In the Common Lectionary and the Lutheran Lectionary the pericope about Jesus' saying on divorce and his blessing of the children are combined in one reading; the Episcopal Lectionary excludes the blessing of the children and the Roman Catholic Lectionary makes the story optional. Both complex stories about Jesus are about the reign of God and about family in relation to God's reign.

The verb *peirazein* (to make trial, to put to the test) certainly in this case means that the Pharisees wanted to trap Jesus; the theme is a familiar one in the Gospels. In Jesus' time the question of divorce was widely debated; strict (Shammai) and lenient (Hillel) views were debated. John the Baptist found himself in political trouble for condemning Herod's divorce, and divorce in the Greco-Roman world was extremely common. In Jewish law, under debate here, only the man could divorce the woman. This suggests that although the issue of divorce had applicability for the whole Mediterranean world of Jesus' time, the wording comes from a Jewish-Christian milieu. The reference in verse 12 implies that it was edited outside of Palestine, because in this region alone women could not obtain a divorce from their husbands.

The passage must be interpreted in light of Jesus' insistence on the absolute standards of the reign of God. Jesus' approach in Mark is apocalyptic, in the sense that Jesus upholds absolute standards, making no provision for the trials and difficulties of life in a very imperfect world.

Jesus holds his contemporaries up to the standards for human life that God envisaged in creation. Moses had allowed exceptions because of human weakness, which appears to include both individual and social/historical human weakness. But Jesus expected God's immanent renewal of creation, and held human beings once again up to God's original ideal.

Of great interest is Jesus' rejection of the absolute authority of Mosaic law (Deut. 24:1-4) as such. Rabbinic authorities debated how to interpret and practice Deuteronomy's legislation about divorce; Jesus used one part of the Torah (Genesis) to cancel another (Deuteronomy). His principle of interpretation is that God's actions set the ideal for human behavior. He attributes Moses' concession of divorce to the Jews' *sklērocardia*—hardness of heart, best interpreted as their unwillingness to be taught by God's will at creation. Thus he presents even a part of the Torah as inferior and to be rejected if it conflicts with a clear expression of God's word for humanity.

In Jesus' description of marriage in verses 6-8, Jesus uses both creation stories, and uses the union of woman and man in marriage not just to support monogamy, as his contemporaries did, but to affirm the indissolubility of marriage. Jesus also makes the obligations of marriage mutual; in his description he gives no hint that the "one flesh" is the male's to control. The marriage union is of two human persons, each equally bound to the other, and each equally required to be faithful to the other. Jesus allows no "double standard."

Verses 10-12 seem to allow divorce but not remarriage for both men and women; this is presented not as a public saying of Jesus, but as a question about a hard case. His response (divorce permitted but not remarriage) suggests that although Jesus' words upheld an absolute and unflinching standard, in practice the early church already by the time of the writing of Mark's Gospel was making exceptions to Jesus' stringent demands (for the sake of human weakness or hardness of heart?). Any exegesis of the passage must recognize that here and in other places the early church recognized the absolute character of Jesus' demands, and also tried to apply his commands to contemporary needs. This church was also struggling with the needs of a church in a world that was lasting longer than Mark's Jesus seemed to expect.

In the deceptively simple story of Jesus' blessing of the little children, which follows the passage on divorce, a clear issue of principle is involved. Jesus is indignant, a word nowhere else used of him. It seems highly unlikely that the dispute with his disciples is merely about the propriety of children on his lap. Themes suggested as being in the writer's mind have included: childhood (however that is defined) as the model for admission into God's domain; Jesus' approval as admitting all, even the weak and marginal, to the reign of God; and a dispute in the early church about infant baptism.

11

HOMILETICAL INTERPRETATION

First Lesson: Genesis 2:18-24. In the context of a liturgy in which the Gospel is read, the first lesson can be the focus of the preaching to ask what ideal God has made central to creation. In some traditions it would be tempting to use this text to expound a natural theology; that seems a misuse liturgically. Rather, the preacher would be more faithful to the obviously intentional matching character of Genesis with the Gospel by exploring the creation account explicitly in context of Jesus' question about marriage.

This reading thus takes its place as an etiology of the relationship between man and woman, their desire for each other (*eros*), and the rooting of that relationship in God's creation. Parallels are present in mythologies of other cultures and traditions; the preacher may or may not want to refer to them (the story of Marduk and Tiamat is always exciting). Since Jesus has conflated the two creation accounts, the preacher focusing on Genesis may want to distinguish this account with its more personal, narrative style from the hieratic reading of the first account.

The real issues internal to the second creation account read today concern the relationship of woman and man, and about marriage. Because this account has been used to defend both the inferiority/subordination of woman to man and the equality of man and woman, the preacher needs to be very clear about the interpretation adopted. Depending on the congregation, the question of the equal humanity of the sexes may be volatile or so accepted as not to seem even necessary of comment.

The preacher may find it helpful to take the congregation carefully through the text, including Adam's search for companionship, with its premises that humans are made to live with each other rather than to be solitary, the creation of the animals who are obviously not adequate companions for Adam, and the final creation of Eve, who is the right one. Adam recognizes Eve as the companion provided by God to be like him and of the same substance as he is. This equality of creation, and origin from the same humanity, is central to Genesis's view of human equality, at least in the garden before the fall. Thus, Genesis claims that God intends equality for humanity, and relationships of subordination and inferiority are expressions of the sinful condition of humanity.

Such an explanation of human relationships is linked clearly by the Jahwist with marriage. The story takes this form: thus God created man and woman, *therefore a* man leaves his father and mother, and cleaves to his wife, and they become one flesh. One cannot ignore the patriarchal slant historically present in the story; all is told from the man's perspective. From the woman's perspective, the good news is that at least in creation, she is not created as chattel or inferior to man, but as equal. The "become[ing] one flesh" does not imply destruction of man's or woman's personhood, but strength in the unity of the two.

In the account, the unity is expressed with the image of "one flesh." This figure is literal, because sexual union is understood to be the sign of their unity. Because flesh means more than bodies, but refers to all dimensions of human existence, the unity is in all dimensions. To explore such an understanding of marriage requires much sensitivity from the preacher. One wants to uphold the desirability of a real communion, but not imply that anyone's individuality ought to be destroyed. Historically, usually the woman's has been under attack. The unity is a community into which people grow through mutual respect, communication, and self-giving to each other. People do not instantaneously become one flesh; it is a process.

This passage and the Gospel are often hostage to the ideology of the moment: the suppression of women's individuality, the condemnation/ exaltation of gay and lesbian relationships, the legal and moral indissolubility of marriage. The preacher ought to be relevant, but she or he needs sensitively to explore the readings for what they say about our life in the light of Scripture, rather than to abuse these readings. If the preacher feels uneasy, or wants to depart too far from the readings, preacher and congregation will particularly benefit from a sermon on Hebrews.

Second Lesson: Hebrews 2:9-11, (12-18). Because the Letter to the Hebrews is in no discernible way connected to the readings from Genesis and Mark, it offers a clear alternative to the preacher who believes that the congregation does not need another sermon about marriage and divorce, or who does not want to preach such a sermon. The next seven weeks offer a *lectio continua* of Hebrews, so the preacher may very well choose to spend much of the sermon time offering some basic background about the letter, its context, and its themes.

Hebrews goes in and out of favor. At the moment it is in eclipse. Its context is not clearly agreed on, its authorship is unknown, and its central imagery of priests, temples, and ritual sacrifice is unpopular in a historical period that is much occupied with human equality and that questions the viability of even the idea of transcendence. One great service the preacher can perform for many a congregation is simply to introduce the epistle and its contributions to Christian life.

Whatever the precise setting, the author encourages in its faith a community that has been persecuted, that sees no end to its troubles, and that wonders if it should continue in its faith or simply return to its old observance of Judaism (probably in a Greek-speaking Jewish context).

Both the praise of the community of faithful believers throughout history (the "cloud of witnesses") and the extended exploration of the person and work of Jesus are intended to rouse the flagging faith of a community.

The preacher today can look at some of those same issues for our time: how we face discouragement, and how the community of faith throughout history and Jesus' own life lifts our faith. Although such themes are not hard to identify or preach about, the presentation of Jesus as priest will not be easy for most contemporary Christians to grasp and find helpful.

Today's reading presents Jesus as both the preexistent one who is God's image, and through whom all was created, thus raising suggestions of neoplatonism or at least the mingling of popular Greek philosophy and Jewish thought. The preacher will need to explore and translate this idea for the congregation. Struggling with the complex notion of incarnation, the author of Hebrews presents his vision of the human Jesus as both the pioneer and perfecter of our faith, and also as the great high priest, atoning for the sins of the people, of whom he is also one. Either of those themes requires a great deal of clear explanation. The preacher cannot assume that many in the congregation will be familiar with either of these themes, and where there is familiarity, such as with atonement, it will generally be distorted and violent.

Especially in nonliturgical churches, the notion of priest will seem quite unfamiliar and disembodied. Because it is a fundamental theme for Hebrews and vitally important for the Christian tradition, the notion of Christ's priesthood should be directly addressed and explored in the sermon. The biblical notion of atonement and its connection with the community of the people might also be a direction to develop.

Gospel: Mark 10:2-16. The Gospel reading is one that makes most moderns uncomfortable. The preacher needs honestly to address that reality. Jesus expresses what sounds like an absolute moral demand, professing the indissolubility of marriage. The sermon may well confront directly the conflict between the desire to hear comforting words from a consoling Jesus, and his demanding statement about marriage and divorce, a reality personally close and emotionally complex for many clergy and laity. Probably for most congregations, as when dealing with all the "hard sayings" of Jesus, it is best to preach directly about the complicated and painful issue.

One approach for the sermon is to put Jesus' words in context of his time. Divorce was a male prerogative in his world. Women could be severely damaged, and had no corresponding rights. Jesus certainly is demanding the return to a higher standard in part as a way of guarding women's dignity. The preacher, however, needs also to recognize that in Mark's

Gospel Jesus expected the world to end soon, and thus in marriage, as with many other human relationships, he held people to the absolute standards of God's realm in expectation that it would soon be realized on earth.

Mark's Gospel already allows an opening, which suggests to us that the church already in his day, facing a long period between Jesus' resurrection and his ascension and his return again, developed ways to allow exceptions to this rigorous standard. Thus the Gospel offers evidence of the church wrestling with the same problem the preacher needs to explore in the sermon: If Jesus expresses an absolute demand, how do (or can) we allow for exceptions? Or must we be literalists and say that if one is married there is no divorce, period? Is the only alternative to say that Jesus erred on this point, and we should just ignore what he said because we have more informed views these days?

The early church allowed divorce without remarriage from Mark's "secret teaching" of Jesus. Paul permitted remarriage if the pagan partner would not let the Christian spouse practice the faith. Over the centuries, churches have developed differing ways to uphold a high standard of marriage, but also to allow some exceptions for human weakness. The Orthodox, for example, allowed divorce and remarriage, but cautiously and with some level of disapproval. The Roman Catholics forbade remarriage after civil divorce, but have interpreted annulment with widely differing degrees of latitude. The preacher might well focus on the church's responsibility, from the biblical period on, to hold to Jesus' very high standard of marriage, but also to make provision for people's mistakes and weakness.

The preacher may also wish to explore how Jesus makes his decision, with his way of interpreting the Scripture. Especially in areas where biblical literalism rules, it may be helpful to point out that Jesus takes two scriptural statements, one from Genesis and the other from Deuteronomy, and makes a judgment between the two where he perceives a conflict. He offers us God's high ideal in creation as our starting point, rather than the socially biased legislation about divorce. Does this offer us any suggestions about how we might make our decisions when we see apparent (or real) conflicts between different parts of the Bible?

If one wanted to preach a less argumentative sermon, one might take Jesus' comment about "hardness of heart" as the reason for the permission for divorce, and seek the positive. If "hardness of heart" causes marriages to fail and necessitates divorce, what are those qualities that enable us to come closer to Jesus' ideal of marriage—the two shall become one flesh? In a broader context, what makes good, unifying relationships, rather than harsh and unhappy relationships that end in one party rejecting the other?

15

Twenty-first Sunday after Pentecost

Lutheran	Roman Catholic	Episcopal	Common Lectionary
Amos 5:6-7, 10-15	Wisd. 7:7-11	Amos 5:6-7, 10-15	Gen. 3:8-19
Heb. 3:1-6	Heb. 4:12-13	Heb. 3:1-6	Heb. 4:1-3, 9-13
Mark 10:17-27 (28-30)	Mark 10:17-30 or 10:17-27	Mark 10:17-27 (28-31)	Mark 10:17-30

EXEGETICAL INTERPRETATION

First Lesson: Genesis 3:8-19; Wisdom 7:7-11; Amos 5:6-7, 10-15.
Today's first lesson offers a fascinating study in the different interpretations a first lesson casts on the Gospel. Although the reading from Genesis in the Common Lectionary is our focus, each of the readings sheds a substantially different light on the Gospel, the story of the rich young ruler. Each lesson gives a distinct interpretive shape.

The lesson from Wisdom in the Roman Catholic Lectionary relates wealth to wisdom, the feminine personification of God's intelligent, creative force in the world. Wisdom is compared to wealth, which fades into utter insignificance beside it. Solomon, the ruler, receives wisdom through prayer, not personal effort. Although he values wisdom far more than any earthly wealth, the passage carefully connects the possession of wisdom with the receiving of wealth. With divine wisdom given to mortals, God will also give wealth. Wisdom is the end to be desired, and wealth is an expected blessing in wisdom's train.

Amos, the selection for the Lutheran and Episcopal lectionaries, identifies a quite different relationship between virtue and wealth. Its prophetic fervor condemns the abuse of wealth, and demands that the people reestablish God's justice in the land. Oppression of the poor for the sake of gain is vehemently condemned. Implicit in the reading is the notion that, contrary to the suggestion in Wisdom, wealth is normally gained through cheating the poor, and thus is almost necessarily morally tainted.

Genesis 3:8-19 is taken from the story of the fall; it begins when Adam and Eve, having eaten of the fruit of the tree of the knowledge of good and evil, hid when they heard the sound of God walking in the garden. The passage bears much theological baggage from Christian speculation about sin and its transmission, and the effects of original sin upon humanity; the preacher does well to try first to understand the passage on its own terms rather than later readings with different historical contexts.

Several themes are woven together: the effects of sin on the individual, on relationship with other individuals, with earth and animals and with God; God's character as just judge; the present order of submission and domination between woman and man as an expression of the effects of sin; and the overwhelming dimension of mortality which colors every aspect of human life.

For homiletical purposes any of these themes could be followed through in detail; the exegetical investigator will need to attend to all of them. A literary analysis is essential. For instance, in light of the Gospel story, one of the most important aspects of the story of the fall is that after Eve and Adam have eaten the fruit, even though they have spoken with God so familiarly, they flee from any encounter with God. By Adam's admission, they are fearful and ashamed. Realizing the effects of the choices they have made, they avoid God's searching scrutiny, because God knows the truth about them. Thus the author of Genesis identifies flight from God, and avoidance of encounter with God's judging truth, as primary characteristics of sinful humanity.

Second Lesson: Hebrews 3:1-6; 4:1-3, 9-13. The second lesson is from the Letter to the Hebrews; in the Lutheran and Episcopal lectionaries Heb. 3:1-6, in the Roman Catholic Heb. 4:12-13, and in the Common Lectionary Heb. 4:1-3, 9-13.

Hebrews 3:1-16 is the opening to the first great section of Hebrews, which acclaims Jesus as the leader of our salvation. The lesson contrasts Moses and Jesus, to show the superiority of Jesus. Both Moses and Jesus are faithful. Moses is faithful as servant *in* God's house; Jesus is faithful as apostle and high priest, the son of God *over* God's house. A formative image of the church for the development of Christian theology occurs in this passage; rather than referring to the church as Body of Christ, as is primary in the Pauline material, Hebrews identifies it as a household/family over which Christ is the head.

In the Common Lectionary, Heb. 4:1-3, 9-13 explores the Christian pilgrimage toward the eternal sabbath rest God has prepared for the people of God. The image of the church predominant in this exhortation is that of the pilgrim people, struggling on the journey through this world, as Israel, the earlier people of God, followed Moses through the wilderness. God's promise of sabbath rest can be fulfilled in the church if they hear the good news with faith, and are obedient to God's word (vv. 1-3, 9-11).

The preacher should note that the verb *eiserchometha* (Heb. 4:3) suggests that our entrance into God's rest is a process in which we are presently engaged, and which will be continued and perfected in eternity. It is also

17

important to note that the author of Hebrews is not specific about what this sabbath rest is. Probably our entrance into rest includes the whole process of salvation, individual and corporate, which is itself our sharing in God's own life. Such a notion has deep and wide roots in Jewish and Greek thought, but most certainly is centered in the image of the God of exodus calling the people from slavery into the freedom of being God's own people.

As if the exhortation about the failure of the people of Israel to obey God and enter into God's rest were not strong enough, verses 12-13 offer a forcible conclusion. God will not be satisfied merely with outward observance, but only with faithfulness in the "thoughts and intentions of the heart." The word of God is compared to a sword, which cuts through all the layers of the person, even to the heart. The rooting of this passage in Wisdom 18:14-16 suggests that the word of God is not only the active command of God, but also the incarnate Word of God, Jesus.

The exhortation is somewhat ambiguous in its warning but it appears that the new people of God are being admonished not to fall short of God's word calling them to obedience, as did the people of Israel. The conclusion to the exhortation is a stern reminder of God's ability to see through all human pretense and disobedience, and lay open the heart to the theme of grace, which will be taken up in the next verses (14-16).

Gospel: Mark 10:17-30. Today's Gospel is paralleled in Matthew and Luke. Mark's is perhaps the strongest and most drastic version of the story. Mark separates this story from the previous tale of the blessing of the children, and introduces the man as someone who approaches Jesus as he is setting out with his disciples. Mark uses none of the descriptive terms Luke and Matthew use; he is simply "a man."

His greeting and posture (kneeling before Jesus) would have appeared extravagant and excessive to a Jewish audience. Perhaps this is why Jesus snaps back: "Why do you call me good: God alone is good," in response to the man's question, "Good Rabbi, what must I do to inherit eternal life?" Preachers have struggled for centuries over the relation of Jesus' comment to the divinity of Jesus; perhaps it is simpler and truer to the situation to hear this exchange as Jesus' reaction to an obsequious questioner. A good Jew would not focus on the teacher, but on God. What does God expect of us if we are to inherit eternal life? Jesus instantaneously moves the action from the stranger's question of him to the question of God's word for humanity.

After the immediate rebuke, Jesus offers the expected answer, bracingly practical and hard: "follow the commandments." After Jesus starts listing them, the man offers the response that changes the direction of the dialogue.

He replies that he has done all these things since his youth. Jesus takes him at his word, assuming the common Jewish teaching that it was possible to be just, to do the works of the Law. The man's rapid response, interrupting Jesus, implies that he wants more, and finds this external obedience inadequate for his religious aspirations.

Jesus' challenge is direct: "You lack one thing: go sell what you possess and give it to the poor, and you will have riches in heaven; and come follow me." Jesus addresses only this man, but in the discussion in verses 23-27 it becomes clear that he is dubious about the possibility of the salvation of the rich. Although common Jewish teaching warned of the danger of riches, it was accepted that wealth could be a blessing enabling one to do good. Jesus advised the young man that he must rid himself of riches because of their danger to him. He will gain treasure in heaven; no social motive is offered for giving. Shedding wealth is an essential part of the path to faithful discipleship.

The man is shocked and leaves; he no longer offers pious accolades to Jesus. The disciples are also taken aback, and in the next verses (23-31) follow the usual pattern in Mark of private teaching and clarification of the disciples following Jesus' public and often puzzling teaching.

The theme of these next verses is that of wealth and renunciation. Verses 23-27 contain Jesus' response to Peter's question: If riches are such a danger, can anyone be saved? Jesus' answer ought not to be cheapened. In the natural course of things, it is impossible, he says. Human acquisitiveness excludes one from the realm of God. But grace makes it possible; God can change the heart even of those who have riches. The phrasing of the response makes clear that Jesus believes that these rich people can be saved even while rich; they do not have to give up everything to follow Jesus. Difficult as it is, God can change their hearts.

Verses 28-30 are only loosely connected to the preceding verses, having in common the reference to riches. It appears to derive from the experience of the early church and the disciples who have given up their own communities and families. Peter poses the question of their reward, and Jesus responds that they will have a reward. God gives them the present community of the church, mixed with the experience of persecutions, and the promise of eternal life. Thus, in a sense, Jesus' answer to Peter completes the response to the rich man. If one is willing to let go of everything to follow Jesus, one will inherit eternal life.

HOMILETICAL INTERPRETATION

First Lesson: Genesis 3:8-19. As was noted in the exegetical interpretation, each of the Old Testament readings casts a quite different interpretation on the Gospel reading. Thus the preacher must first decide which of the texts will provide the focus for preaching. The story about Adam and Eve expresses very clearly the web that sin weaves about us, limiting and falsifying our ability to decide and make choices. That unquestionably is one aspect of the Gospel reading and can be preached in connection with it; Genesis can also provide its own homily about Adam and Eve.

The preacher who chooses to focus on the passage itself would do well to offer some of the immediate background from the Jahwist creation story, and some perspective on the enormity of the decision made by the first humans to eat the fruit of the tree of the knowledge of good and evil. The tale itself can be interpreted on the psychological level and the theological; probably the preacher needs to attend to both.

Centuries of Christian tradition read debates about original sin and human sinfulness into the Genesis account; the Jewish tradition does not see sinfulness as so dominant a theme or as such a central aspect of human character as the Christian tradition has read it in Genesis 3. In the story we do see, however, wide-ranging effects of human disobedience to God: inability to face God, refusal to take personal responsibility, and placing of blame on others.

The present world order of domination of man over woman and of male servitude to unrelenting labor for survival is presented as an inherently sinful one, which has arisen because of human sin. These orders, which in some traditions become understood as a "natural order," are in Genesis presented as "unnatural" for creation. They are imposed on Adam and Eve as a result of sin. Thus whenever deliverance or redemption comes to humanity, one would expect this punishing order to be lifted.

One might read this passage, asking, "What is the effect of sin, and what would people not shaped by sin be like?" Such people certainly would assume responsibility for their actions, speak and respond directly to God's call, not be ashamed of direct exposure to God and to others, find labor a joy and delight, and never dominate one over the other. People in fact behave quite differently, and the author of this part of Genesis regards that irresponsible and oppressive behavior as sinful.

As one extends the Genesis reading to the Gospel, the behavior of the man who addresses Jesus is clearly that of one dominated by sin. He is so trapped by his wealth that he cannot let go of it even for a direct command of God spoken through God's appointed teacher to him. He refuses to take responsibility and act as he is being called to do, even in the light of the mortality of his own condition and the short life of riches. In this regard, the pattern of Adam and Eve's behavior repeats itself in their children.

Second Lesson: Hebrews 4:1-3, 9-13. Any sermon about the second reading must, as is usually the case, express a different line of thought from the Gospel pericope. (Today's lectionary offers an even clearer example of the discontinuity of the readings: the Episcopal and Lutheran selection from Hebrews is quite discontinuous with the Roman Catholic Lectionary and the Common Lectionary.) Hebrews 4 focuses on faithful discipleship and the metaphor of the Christian life as pilgrimage.

Any preacher, however, who attempts to connect the reading from Hebrews with the Gospel treads on very thin ice. Better to choose to focus on one or other of the readings, even if one might make a connection with the theme of discipleship. Instead, one might offer a rich sermon about an aspect of the Christian life seldom addressed from the pulpit.

This section of the letter discusses the image of Christian life as pilgrimage and the end of the pilgrimage as entering into the rest that God promised to our ancestors. In a society that does not know how to enjoy leisure, much less rest with contentment and peace, the very notion of rest, and especially rest in God, will require much exploration. Rest as a condition of trust in God and abandonment of self to God without struggle or effort will be a strange idea to many people. Yet there will be situations where this sort of sermon will be very welcome to people as a goal to which we are moving in our relationship to God.

Besides exploring the interior aspects of rest, the externals may also be a good focus for the preacher. "Sabbath rest" is a foretaste of the peace of our relationship with God, and our rest in God. Several modern writers have touched on our loss in giving up an environment of sabbath rest in our struggle to rid ourselves of some of the artificiality of situations in which people were forbidden to enjoy themselves rather than encouraged to enjoy an anticipation of rest with God and each other.

The famous metaphor of God's Word as a two-edged sword can be used to explore the interiority of our relationship with God, and the radical openness that God's Word can bring to us. The Word of God of which the author of Hebrews writes is not the abstraction "Scripture is the authoritative Word of God." The Word is God's living spirit, which can discern all our intentions and thoughts. The graphic image of knife or sword, slicing through flesh with ease and accuracy, is a mere hint of the ways in which God can expose our true thoughts and intentions, as distinct from our self-presentation. The author introduces the notion of God as judge to reinforce the idea that God's Word truly exposes us to ourselves and to others.

A sermon focusing on this reading would need to be very specific. The point of the last few verses is that "we read most books; the Scripture reads us." How does the Scripture read us? How does the Scripture interpret, judge, advise, give perspective? Examples from individual and community life abound, but need to be explicitly offered to the congregation.

The preacher will also want to make an explicit connection between the earthly pilgrimage, sabbath rest, and the truth for repentance and reform that is an essential concomitant of our earthly pilgrimage toward our rest in God. This connection will also need to be very specific, concrete, and contemporary.

Gospel: Mark 10:17-30. This reading from Mark's Gospel can be approached by the preacher in various ways. The story itself is gripping, with the obsequious religious seeker flattering Jesus, Jesus' crisp and demanding response, the man's immediate lack of interest in responding to the challenge Jesus laid before him, and Jesus' warning to the disciples about the spiritually destructive effects of wealth, and their special need of God's grace to disentangle them from the love of riches.

An effective sermon flows from a thoughtful exploration of each development in this story, and a careful probing of the internal drama of the rich man's futile struggle for mastery over his own soul. Mark presents a stark tale, with a strong warning about the danger of wealth because of its effect on people.

The preacher may choose to focus quite directly on the classical religious notion of detachment. The man is tangled up in his own wealth. Jesus delivers an ultimatum to him—give it all up. Jesus does not, as the commentators note, suggest this gesture for the good of the poor, but for the rich man's sake. For his own spiritual integrity, he must get rid of his earthly treasures and have only heavenly treasure. Even later on, when Jesus addresses the disciples in verses 28-30, they are offered the goods of this world only after they have given up family and possessions.

The pericope does not suggest that salvation can come only if one embraces physical poverty, but, as seen in Jesus' words to the rich man and to the disciples, one must give up all sense of ownership of anything. All belongs to God, and the children of God's realm on earth will receive what they need in this life, and eternal life in the next. But they will also be persecuted—with the threat of loss of goods, family, and life which persecution meant for the early church.

For most congregations, this could be a thought-provoking starting point for a thorough exploration of the spirituality of stewardship. We must be ready to give up everything—and sometimes even act on that readiness. The preacher may wish to cast a look back at Genesis to explore the human tendency to grab everything for oneself, abandon responsibility, and blame others. To discipline oneself, and to express one's total faith in God, one must give up everything—even if as a disciple one receives it back from God. All is God's.

This message probably will be much more difficult to receive than the usual (and very true!) stewardship sermons that encourage congregants to give because of gratitude, or to fulfill a biblical standard. Jesus' approach in this reading pushes to the limits of the human heart and will.

Twenty-second Sunday after Pentecost

Lutheran	Roman Catholic	Episcopal	Common Lectionary
Isa. 53:10-12	Isa. 53:10-11	Isa. 53:4-12	Isa. 53:7-12
Heb. 4:9-16	Heb. 4:14-16	Heb. 4:12-16	Heb. 4:14-16
Mark 10:35-45	Mark 10:35-45 or 10:42-45	Mark 10:35-45	Mark 10:35-45

EXEGETICAL INTERPRETATION

First Lesson: Isaiah 53:10-12. Although even today a few authors argue for the unity of the prophecy of Isaiah, differences of language and theme point to two or three authors of the biblical book and at least two distinct times of composition. Our reading for this Sunday is from that part of the book commonly called Second Isaiah. First Isaiah is ordinarily identified as chapters 1–39, dated around the late eighth and early seventh centuries B.C.E., and Second Isaiah as chapters 40–66, from about a century and a half later. Some scholars would distinguish a Third Isaiah, chapters 56–66, dated from about 540–500 B.C.E.

The theme of the servant of Yahweh is one that distinguishes Second Isaiah from First Isaiah, where it does not appear at all. At different times in the four songs of the servant, the servant is portrayed as an individual, at other times as the idealized nation, and sometimes the identity is left ambiguous. Christians and Jews have thus interpreted the passage quite differently. The Jewish tradition has identified the servant historically (Moses, Job, and Cyrus have been suggested); eschatologically (the Messiah); or allegorically (the ideal Israel, or an elite among Israel). From its earliest preaching the Christian community saw explicitly in the servant songs a prophecy of Jesus as the agent of God's redemptive work among the nations.

In the Jewish interpretative tradition, the servant often is both a collective ideal of Israel and a model for personal behavior. The Christian exegesis points to the messianic figure of Jesus and his atoning life, although the notion of an individual's imitation of Christ as the suffering servant is also present in the tradition.

The fourth song of the servant extends from 52:13—53:12, but the pericope for today is much shorter (Roman Catholic 53:10-11; Lutheran 53:10-12; Common Lectionary 53:7-12; Episcopal 53:4-12). The lesson is intended to offer an Old Testament comment on the Gospel reading, in which Jesus teaches about the nature of servanthood in the community of faith. In response to James' and John's request, Jesus asserts that his own (messianic) ministry is that of a servant, not a monarch, and that leadership among the disciples takes the character of mutual service and humility. Thus Jesus' own interpretation of the servant figure in Isaiah seems to be both messianic and moral, reflecting the ideal of the realm of God he has come to proclaim.

Verses 1-3 of the servant song express the humiliation of the servant and his rejection by the nations. Verses 4-6 portray the vicarious character of the servant's suffering, which atones for all the people, both Israel and the Gentiles, all of whom have sinned. Verses 7-9 describe the silent suffering of the servant, who is executed because of the sins of the people and buried among the wicked, despite his innocence. Verses 10-12 describe the vindication of the servant, who is delivered from death by God and returned to life because he was willing to become an offering for the people's sin.

Many are made righteous because of the suffering of the righteous servant. "Many" was interpreted as "all" by some of the later rabbis, giving the passage a universal tone; in the Christian tradition the universal effect of Jesus' death and resurrection is read into this passage.

Second Lesson: Hebrews 4:14-16. The Roman Catholic and the Episcopal lectionaries include parts of Hebrews 4 leading up to these verses; please see the exegesis of last week's verses for specific references. Hebrews 4:14-16 articulates the themes of moving forward, a consistent refrain in Hebrews; looking back to Jesus as pioneer, faithful servant, and Son, greater than Moses; and resuming and elaborating the role of Jesus as the great High Priest. These verses present Jesus' progress as High Priest as a movement forward in his redemptive work, which empowers us, his followers, also to move forward toward God, who offers us mercy and grace.

The term "great high priest" in verse 14 is probably a reflection of traditional language: the Hebrew for the high priest (*kohen gadol*) was translated into Greek as great priest (*archiereus megas*). Unquestionably in the early Christians' minds Jesus was the great High Priest in the sense in which Hebrews affirms, high priest of a greater and different order than the high priests of the old covenant. Much of the rest of the letter is devoted to the development of the superiority of Jesus' high priesthood, and its consequences for us.

According to common Jewish lore, there were seven heavens before God's throne was reached. The rationale ("since we have") for Jesus' superiority is introduced here by the assertion that he has not passed through the veil

24

of the earthly temple into the Holy of Holies as does the Jewish high priest, but has "passed through" the heavens to God's throne itself. The progress of Jesus is not the sort of passage one finds in some gnostic literature, in which the savior figure travels from or through hostile territory to the highest heavens, but rather in the excellence of Jesus who has such cosmic power and is able to reach God's throne itself.

Because we have such a superior high priest, Christians thus are motivated to "hold fast to our confession" of faith. This assertion of the need to hold fast to what has been received balances the other theme of movement forward, so that the believer is portrayed as one who both possesses a sure and certain reality, and is also (and therefore) able to move forward in earthly pilgrimage toward God. "Because we have a great high priest . . . therefore let us move forward."

Verses 15-16 present the same sort of relationship between the quality of Jesus' high priesthood and our sinfulness. Because *(gar)* we have a High Priest who has been tested as we are, yet is without sin . . . therefore *(oun)* let us approach the throne of grace. Our movement and access to God are dependent on Jesus' preceding us and making our movement possible.

Verse 15 is very difficult for modern psychologically minded Christians, who want access to Jesus' interior life to know if he had all kinds of temptations, especially sexual ones. The assumption is that Jesus could not have been human if he had not sinned, because sin is an essential part of human consciousness. What the author of Hebrews seems to mean by without sin, in this context, however, is rather more like what Wesley meant by perfection.

"Without sin" refers to Jesus' faithfulness referred to earlier in the letter, his incarnation for the purpose of doing God's will. In contrast to our need for psychological dramatic tension, neither the Jewish nor Hellenistic religious worlds could have imagined portraying a savior as sinful, that is, as being in conflict with the divine will for the world.

The figure of the sinless great High Priest who advances through the heavens to the throne of God is expanded in verse 16, which is the moral exhortation addressed to the Christian community. The throne of grace evokes the image of God's heavenly throne that is on earth in the Holy of Holies in the temple in Jerusalem, into which the High Priest enters on the Day of Atonement. Because the Christian has such access to God now, past sins may be forgiven and grace is available to the present and future.

Gospel: Mark 10:35-45. Mark's Gospel presents James and John as the key figures in evoking from Jesus strong statements about his own ministry and its character as a servant ministry. The dialogue recounted takes place immediately after Jesus' prediction that the Son of man must go to Jerusalem to suffer and die there (vv. 32-34). The juxtaposition of these two narratives implies that the disciples have once again failed to understand the meaning of Jesus' life and ministry, and still seek earthly glory and power. Two stories are joined together here to illuminate Jesus' teaching about the reign of God, power, and discipleship.

James and John are presented as coming forward to beg Jesus for special treatment. The episode is discreditable to them; perhaps its use reflects a later effort to minimize their importance. Their question is a typical request such as might be made of the leader in a system that depended on maneuvering for power and precedence. They ask Jesus if they can be the chief leaders of his messianic leadership group (the new Sanhedrin) in the new age. Their model is clearly that of the new Israel as a political realm, based on earthly power to dominate and control. The anger of the disciples referred to in verse 41 assures us that the other disciples so understood their efforts.

Jesus' response to them in verses 38-40 reflects a natural response. They have requested status in the future messianic realm, but such dominion is not Jesus' to give. (This reminds us of Jesus' retort to the rich man in verse 18.) Instead, Jesus offers them what he can—they will be able to follow him on earth in the path of suffering he has described in verses 33-34. In the Old Testament, "drinking the cup" was used of both intense good or painful experiences. Being overcome by many waters is a frequent phrase for great suffering and distress in the Psalms; in common Greek to be baptized (*baptizesthai*) expressed that same sentiment.

In verses 42-45 Jesus, perhaps detecting the depth of feeling evoked by power struggles in communities, calls the disciples together to clarify his notions of discipleship and authority. Rulership among the Gentiles, he says, addressing the ideal of power in his day, takes tyranny and dominance as its model. Jesus, with strong hyperbole, places a totally different image before the disciples. Power comes from service (*diakonia*), he asserts, and the ruler must become a slave (*doulos*).

Jesus gives this vigorously delineated model its context by referring the hearer back to Mark 8:31, and to the image of the servant in Isaiah 53. The servant's willingness to be faithful to his mission even unto persecution and death not only gains the servant life, but is redemptive and atoning for the people. In these verses and reference back to the prophet's words, Jesus sets up a quite different model of power from any popular then or now.

HOMILETICAL INTERPRETATION

First Lesson: Isaiah 53:10-12. In the Christian homiletical tradition, it is virtually impossible to separate the Christian application of the servant songs to Jesus from their meaning in Isaiah. Such use of the texts, particularly in the Passion narratives, is found within the New Testament itself. Any effort to treat in depth the Isaian material separately will be virtually useless in the pulpit; the congregation will consciously or unconsciously connect the Isaian prophecy with Jesus in the Gospels. To justify to a congregation separating the two readings and preaching with the focus on Isaiah in its own context is a sermon in itself.

Gospel: Mark 10:35-45. Thus homiletically the first reading and the Gospel passage are particularly closely intertwined. The great issue raised in the Gospel is, What is the character of leadership among God's people? Both in the period of second Isaiah and Mark's Gospel the community had to struggle with the reality of a harsh and oppressive civil government. As always, as the Gospel story illustrates, the church's temptation is uncritically to model its leadership along secular lines.

James and John vociferously demand the rights of leadership along their idealized secular model, and the other disciples respond, not by critiquing their idea of leadership, but by trying to outmaneuver them at their own game. Jesus, however, offers a radical critique. His model of leadership depends neither on possession and control, nor on rejection of the world. Rather, he offers service and self-sacrifice as the values animating the leadership he wants for his own community. In his own day, as we see from the disciples' reactions, Jesus' vision was countercultural. It is also in our own day, but for some slightly different reasons.

Domination, control, and superiority of one over another are all constants in human behavior. Only the values or achievements that give one person power over another differ from time to time and place to place. Jesus attacks the very justification of human domination. As one theologian remarked, Jesus does not teach that we are all equal to each other, but something far more radical. Jesus asserts that every human being is of infinite value. Because of the infinite value of each human before God, we are expected to treat each other with infinite respect. Servanthood is an essential (if not the only) metaphor to express our relationship to each other in God's realm.

The preacher knows, and probably must acknowledge, that neither the world nor the church (local, national, or international) functions that way. To the extent that we do not, we are not following the biblical model of servant leadership as exemplified in the servant songs, and personified for us in Jesus. We are just as unfaithful, fearful, and ignorant as Jesus' disciples two thousand years ago.

Thus much of the sermon may well explore what servanthood means for a Christian. The preacher will want to examine false models of human

27

relations held up before us and then direct our attention to servanthood as expressed in Isaiah and in Jesus' response to the disciples. The biblical ideal of mutual servanthood in our relationships is both an ideal and a corrective to oppressive and domineering behavior. In this context, the preacher must also honestly and calmly acknowledge the false and manipulative uses of ideals of service and self-sacrifice to justify religiously the oppression of powerless people.

Feminist and African American theologians have pointed to their experience that the preaching of servanthood has almost exclusively come from representatives of the political and religious establishment. Whether intended (as often was obviously the case) or not, such preaching often reinforced in the powerless among the congregation the conviction that they ought not to exercise their will or judgment, and simply do what they were told to do by their masters or superiors.

Probably the most effective approach to counteract such misuse is to focus very carefully on what Jesus means by servanthood—to explore the suffering servant in Isaiah and then in Jesus' own understanding of obedience to God, even to death. Service is thus not merely to do what people want you to do. Sometimes God's servant will have to do things that displease others very much, challenging their needs or expectations. Such behavior is servant behavior in the biblical sense when it is faithful to God's Word, and is intended to draw people into God's realm.

In Isaiah the servant is "despised"; that theme continues in the Gospel reading. The disciple who is God's servant serves others in God's name, for God's sake. Thus one serves others for God's purposes, not as the pawn of warring, controlling interests. The preacher will want to hold up for the congregation the interconnection between servanthood and the struggle to bring about the realm of God on earth.

Because the passage is so easy to misinterpret, it is extremely important that the preacher offer specific examples of servant behavior and leadership. What does it mean to be a servant? What are some examples from individual and corporate life of a religious and of a more secular nature? What are the costs as well as the rewards of such a life? What are some points of connection as well as tension with contemporary society?

Second Lesson: Hebrews 4:14-16. As frequently happens, the preacher must choose between a sermon about the first reading and the Gospel or about the Letter to the Hebrews. Especially this week, there is no real interconnection between these readings. The theme of Hebrews is the excellence of Jesus' high priesthood, with particular focus on Jesus as the sinless High Priest through whom we receive mercy and grace from God. For most moderns, the theology here is incomprehensible at first glance.

The preacher can provide a helpful service by illuminating for people the theological themes of the letter.

The author of the letter explores in great detail the issue of Jesus' high priesthood and the importance of that priesthood for us. In Hebrews, Jesus' faithfulness is the motivation and encouragement for the Christian community's faithfulness. The reference, therefore, to Jesus' passage through the heavens is not about aerodynamic achievements or even gnostic triumphs over hostile worlds, but an expression of Jesus' continuing pilgrimage and pioneering for us. The central motif of his incarnation and progress in this life and through the cosmos back to the throne of God is boundless faithfulness to God. Through his faithfulness, we, his brothers and sisters, are brought into his community, into the heavenly city.

Our psychological age, including most of the people present in the congregation, will hear the phrase "without sin" not as praise of Jesus, but as a stumbling block. How can someone who has not struggled and fallen really understand our human condition? The preacher may best respond to that objection by noting that sin in the Letter to the Hebrews means unfaithfulness to God's purposes—rather like Wesley's concept of perfection.

Following Wesley's interpretation, sinlessness means a fundamental adherence to God—a consistent, lifelong willingness to do God's will and an equally stable attitude of refusal to do what seems to be in contradiction to God's purposes. The author of Hebrews probably would never have asked about whether Jesus felt sexual urges, was impatient, angry, and so forth. The relevant question was, Was Jesus always trying to do God's will? The answer "yes" is equivalent to sinlessness. The very notion of Jesus as savior is incompatible, in the author's mind, with unfaithfulness to God.

In verse 16, the throne of grace recalls the Old Testament Ark of the Covenant. In this case, however, the Christian who follows Jesus is assured that through Jesus' faithfulness the believer can now come near to God and share in God's favor. For the contemporary congregation, the question is not so much about the distance between God and ourselves as it is about whether there is a God who cares about us. The resounding message of Hebrews is that God is a God of mercy and grace. By faith we see Jesus as both the expression of God's mercy to us, and the one who leads us to God's mercy. The preacher might thus preach about the God to whom Jesus leads us, as portrayed in Hebrews, distinguished from contemporary images of a divinity who is a power of nature, or a mere name for chance.

Twenty-third Sunday after Pentecost

Lutheran	Roman Catholic	Episcopal	Common Lectionary
Jer. 31:7-9	Jer. 31:7-9	Isa. 59:9-19	Jer. 31:7-9
Heb. 5:1-10	Heb. 5:1-6	Heb. 5:12—6:1, 9-12	Heb. 5:1-6
Mark 10:46-52	Mark 10:46-52	Mark 10:46-52	Mark 10:46-52

EXEGETICAL INTERPRETATION

First Lesson: Jeremiah 31:7-9. Jeremiah the prophet began his ministry about 623 B.C.E., and continued until an unknown time after the conquest and exile of the people of Judah by the Babylonians in 587–586 B.C.E. According to tradition, he died some time after 587 in Egypt.

Thus, during his life he experienced some of the most painful moments of Judah's history; much of his prophetic ministry was devoted to calling the people to repentance and to submission to God's judgment on them for their sinfulness. They especially resented his preaching that Judah ought to submit to the power of Babylon, rather than making a proud and foolish alliance with Egypt. Consequently he experienced much persecution by those who opposed his perceived meddling in politics and his attacks on the reformed cultus in the temple resulting from Josiah's reforms; he was arrested just before the fall of Jerusalem and at other times attempts were made on his life.

The so-called Book of Consolation (Jeremiah 30–31), appears to be interjected amid historical and autobiographical material about the conquest and exile. Verses 7-9 describe, in words not unrelated to Isaiah's, the return of the exiles to a restored Jerusalem. Some scholars have attacked the authenticity of this oracle because of its similarity to the Isaiah consolation material, while others have argued that dependence on a common source explains the relationship. Substantial authenticity seems plausible because God's fidelity and keeping of promises was one of Jeremiah's major themes in his preaching and prophetic actions.

God's undying mercy is probably the dominant theological theme of Jeremiah's prophecies. The mention of the blind man in the Gospel story of the healing of Bartimaeus is related specifically to the mention of the return of the blind in the restoration of Israel. In Jeremiah's prophecy, the preceding verses contain God's expression of undying love. God's faithful

30

love (*hesed*) is the reason why Israel shall be restored to the fruitful land, and festive pilgrimages to the Jerusalem temple will be resumed. In verses 7-9, God calls upon the people to sing praise for the restoration of the whole community of Israel, including the most helpless.

We may imagine, as the prophet would have us do, a great procession of people from all over the Mediterranean world where the Israelites and Judeans have been exiled. The great company is not just of warriors or wealthy courtiers, but prominently includes the most helpless of the people: blind, lame, pregnant women—the most vulnerable and handicapped in traveling. So great is God's power that even they can travel home easily and happily. In words reminiscent of Psalm 126:6-7, the people return weeping, while God consoles the exiles and brings them back by the easy road with straight ways and brooks of water by the path. This return from exile, God is careful to say, is for all of the people, Israel and Judah, north and south.

The tenor of the reading from Isaiah 59:9-19, which is used in the Episcopal readings, is quite different. It contrasts the people's lack of justice with God's own righteousness, which strikes down God's adversaries in order to do justice. God's enemies will learn to fear God's justice, which is effective as human injustice is not. Its relationship to the Gospel reading seems to be the identification of God's justice as the active agent in vindicating the righteous.

Second Lesson: Hebrews 5:1-6, (7-10).   The Lutheran, Roman Catholic, and Common Lectionaries use this passage in Hebrews; the Episcopal Lectionary explores a quite different theme in Hebrews 5:12—6:1, 9-12. Hebrews 5 treats the question of how Jesus as the High Priest is able to sympathize with sinful humanity. The author addresses the central theme of the epistle: Jesus' high priesthood and atoning work for us.

In this passage and throughout the whole Letter to the Hebrews, there is no direct reference to recent or contemporary Jewish life of the writer's time, with the temple cultus and the high priesthood. All the references to priesthood are to the Old Testament, particularly to the Torah. This phenomenon casts doubt on interpretations that try to prove this letter is directed to a primarily Jewish audience, or at least suggest that it is directed to those whose measure of truth is the Bible, not contemporary Jewish practice.

The high priest, according to the author, addressing the qualities of a leader for salvation, fulfills the following characteristics: He is a human being and therefore can represent humanity; he is compassionate and shares our weakness; he is appointed to this office by God. These characteristics are important, because the author of Hebrews wants to show that Jesus' high priesthood fulfills these biblical criteria, at the same time that Jesus and his work are greater than the Jewish high priest.

The atoning sacrifices the high priest offers are for "the ignorant and the erring," because the Old Testament provides no sacrifices for deliberate sin. This inadequacy provides another area where Jesus supersedes the sacrificial system of the old law. Jesus' sacrifice is effective for all sin. Jesus' sacrifice is effective for all, and Jesus is able to be sympathetic to all because of his sharing of the human condition, not because of his own inadequacy in following God. Thus, Jesus' sacrifice is purely for others, the human race of whom God gave Jesus charge (v. 1).

Verses 5-6 elaborate v. 4, which describes the high priesthood as an honor which one receives from God, but would not dare take oneself. Aaron is referred to in v. 4, not as the origin of Jesus' priesthood, but as an example of one who is called by God rather than seeking the office. The citations from the Psalms in 5-6 refer to the christological foci of Hebrews.

Psalm 2:7 is cited in the Gospel accounts of Jesus' baptism, and Ps. 110:4 connects Jesus with an eternal priesthood like that of Melchizedek. (Hebrews 1–10 offers an interpretation of Melchizedek's priesthood that exalts it over the levitical priesthood.) Thus, Jesus is portrayed in his high priesthood as the preexistent son, sent from God, as both ruler and priest.

Jesus is not simply someone "just like us," but the eternally preexisting beloved of God who is sent by God to do God's redeeming work in the world, and returns the world to its relationship with God through his freely offered sacrifice of himself in faithful obedience. Verses 7-10 expand and deepen the treatment of Jesus' incarnate life as sacrificial and redemptive for humanity.

Hebrews 5:12—6:1, 9-12, used in the Episcopal Lectionary, addresses the moral dimension of the community to whom Hebrews is addressed. Apparently they have fallen from their high promise in the beginning of their Christian life and "become dull in understanding." The author calls them to rise above the basics of the Christian life, and quicken their fervor in living a faithful Christian life.

Gospel: Mark 10:46-52. Today's Gospel is an important transition point in the structure of Mark's Gospel, as well as functioning as an important teaching story in the early church. In Mark 8:22-26, another story of Jesus healing a blind man is recounted, to begin the middle section of the Gospel, which examines Jesus' identity and the disciples' inability to understand. These healing stories serve as literary markers, ironic comments on the disciples' own blindness, and reminders that God alone can give insight into the mystery of Jesus' person and work.

This Gospel account is settled very precisely near the conclusion of the journey of Jesus and the disciples to Jerusalem. Jerusalem is the locus for opposition to Jesus and his mission; thus the story both concludes the teaching about and exploring of Jesus' identity, and connects the middle section of the Gospel with the drama of the last week of Jesus' life, beginning with his messianic entry into Jerusalem. Herodian Jericho, of Jesus' day, is slightly west of Old Testament Jericho, into the river valley.

On the eve of his entry into Jerusalem, Jesus encounters a blind man, called Bartimaeus. Because in Aramaic this word means Son of Timaeus, scholars have debated whether this name is authentic and part of an eyewitness account of a healing, or whether this is a later addition taken from the name of Bartimaeus of Jerusalem, follower of Jesus. Although it is tempting to assert that the little touches like a proper name signify an identifiable individual known to the author, it seems safer to say that we only know that the author ascribes this name to the blind man.

The personality of the blind man emerges very strongly. He is bold, demanding, persistent, and trusting in Jesus' effectiveness. This tale is the only open acclamation of Jesus as the Messiah before his entry into Jerusalem (11:9-11); it signals a new stage in Jesus' acceptance of his role. The bystanders' efforts to silence the man are made because his hailing Jesus as the Son of David could be construed as treason by a nervous government.

His pleas to Jesus to "have mercy on me" add a different note to his request; they are words of prayer to God, and not appropriate to a civil ruler. Certainly in the Gospel, the intention is that the blind man (who is ironically portrayed as "seeing" Jesus' true identity more clearly than the disciples) hail Jesus in his true messianic identity, as the bearer of the new age, in which God will restore all things.

Jesus does not rebuke or silence him, which indicates that now Jesus is ready for public recognition of his true identity, and also ready to challenge the Jerusalem authorities and accept his fate at their hands when and if they reject his preaching. Once Jesus calls the man, the bystanders are pictured as encouraging him, and he eagerly springs forth. A variant reading describes him as putting on his cloak, which would have been spread around him to receive the coins of the passersby. The most common version, however, describes him springing up to reach Jesus, and from the very earliest periods he has been presented in Christian catechesis as the model of Christian enthusiasm in responding to God's call.

Jesus uses no gestures or signs, merely telling him that he is healed through his faith. He then immediately receives his sight and follows Jesus. The phrase *en tē odō* (in the way), can mean to physically follow Jesus on the journey to Jerusalem, but it can also mean to become a follower of Jesus' way of life, and thus it was understood in the early Christian community. The story of Bartimaeus became a catechetical and homiletic focus for the progress of grace in the believer: humble supplication of Jesus, eager response to Jesus' call, and faithful discipleship.

HOMILETICAL INTERPRETATION

First Lesson: Jeremiah 31:7-9.   The reading for today belies the prophet's popular reputation for doom and gloom. The theme of God's fidelity and fulfillment of promises is as strong in the prophet's proclamation of God's word as the warning to the people. Even though some have questioned the authenticity of these verses, the concrete and vivid portrayal of the people's return from exile is utterly consistent with the faith of that same prophet who purchased a field on the eve of the Babylonian invasion.

In these few verses two equally strong themes complement each other: First, God's promises will be fulfilled; and second, God especially protects the vulnerable. God's fidelity is at the heart of Jeremiah's words to the people. If his warnings sound loud and forceful, it is only because he is utterly convinced that God loves Israel and lives in a covenant relationship with the nation. Such love is strong, generous, and demanding. God may punish Israel for its treacherous and disloyal behavior, but God will never abandon the people. God remains always faithful, waiting and hoping for the people to respond to the eternal invitation.

Side by side with this essential component of Jeremiah's theology is another element fundamental to the prophetic tradition. Today we might express it in such terms as "God's preferential option for the poor." Jeremiah, as other prophets, expressed the thought more concretely and perhaps with less room for misunderstanding, in terms later to be woven into the Magnificat.

God, according to the prophet, will save the poor, the remnant, those who have no one else to protect them. Great bas-reliefs on ancient palace walls portray the horrors of the forced marches of those conquered and resettled by the Babylonians and the Assyrians. The strong would suffer greatly; many of the weak, women, and children must have perished along the way. Such marches were a major expression of the absolute power of an unfeeling empire, willing to dislocate and destroy those who opposed it.

The return from exile is God's merciful deliverance from such earthly tyranny. God's promise is fulfilled when the displaced return to their homes in a progress that protects and prospers even the weakest. God's standards are not those of earthly empire, but those of parental protection and love. Thus, unlike the generals supervising the forced marches, God directs all for the people's good and for the benefit of the most helpless—the blind, the lame, the pregnant women.

Thus, the element of surprise is a strong one in Jeremiah's preaching, and transfers well to our day, to a society that is equally enamored of power, wealth, strength, and physical beauty. God's standards are very different, and flow from God's love for the people, rather than God's needs or desires to gain from them. A good prophetic sermon would probe God's ideals for society as compared to those of the contemporary social structure.

Second Lesson: Hebrews 5:1-6, (7-10).   The Common Lectionary reading, Hebrews 5:1-6, continues last week's reading from Hebrews. That part of the letter wrestled with fidelity and sinfulness. This week's continues that theme, but introduces a new note of complexity, that of Jesus' special relationship to God.

Very few people would quarrel with an assertion that Jesus was a noble and wise teacher, a human being of high moral standards, and a good model for human beings. But many, even among Christians, would not venture further. Jesus is like us, but better, just as we would be if we would try harder to be good.

But the theology of the Letter to the Hebrews differs from that view. Jesus is like us in all things, but Jesus is also "chosen among the people." The two references in the Psalms, regardless of their original meaning, are used in Hebrews to point to a messianic and priestly role of Jesus that is God-given. It exalts him because of God's choice. It is precisely because Jesus is like us, but not just like us, that he is the mediator of redemption to us.

Depending on the particular congregation and its beliefs, the preacher could take this opportunity to explore different Christologies, and some of the different consequences of the various theories. For instance, in the Christology of Hebrews, the humble becoming flesh of the heavenly Son is redemptive, enabling Jesus to be pioneer and intercessor, leading us to restored communion with God. None of these notions is common or even initially comprehensible to most contemporary Christians. A preacher who could make those ideas clear and even appealing for a congregation would be offering a great service. Whether or not people accept the theology, they will have increased their appreciation and understanding for the mainstream of Christian orthodoxy about the divine–human relationship and the process of redemption.

Gospel: Mark 10:46-52.   Today's Gospel story offers a charming and vivid tale of Jesus and his disciples on the road leaving Jericho. The irony of the story is worthy of the preacher's attention. Now, as Jesus goes to Jerusalem to face the authorities, he accepts the acclaim that before he silenced from the mouths of his disciples. The blind man cries out to Jesus, using a messianic title, and Jesus accepts it without challenging or demurring.

The evangelist seemingly revels in the irony of the blind Bartimaeus acclaiming Jesus while the sighted and presumably learned miss the truth about Jesus: He is the Messiah whom they have been seeking. Two aspects of irony that might be productive for the preacher are especially emphasized in Mark's story. First, the blind see and the sighted are blind (to the deeper truth). Exploration of that possibility in the life of the individual, the congregation, or the wider community can allow unsettling possibilities to be considered. Second, the acclamation of Jesus' true character comes close to the time of his passion and death. Part of the messianic secret seems to be that it can only be revealed and understood in perspective of the passion and resurrection.

The classical catechetical interpretation of the figure of Bartimaeus is also a very productive one for the preacher. Bartimaeus is quite intentionally portrayed in Mark as the model for the one who seeks Jesus—admitting blindness, seeking help, eager, faithful, and obedient in discipleship. Part of the perspective of this story is overtly the early Christian terminology for baptism—*photismos,* illumination. In the liturgical world of the hearers of Mark's Gospel, the catechumen is the blind person who comes to Jesus to be enlightened. Baptism is the admission to a new relationship to Jesus, in which one receives light so as to experience God and the world in new light, with a new relationship. The catechumen hears the gospel to prepare for baptism; the baptized listen to the gospel and are reminded of the grace of baptism they have received.

The pattern of Bartimaeus's healing testifies to the ideal pattern of Christian initiation, in which faith is the key to response to Jesus. Faith leads the beggar to call Jesus and to respond with a demand for healing/redemption. Once Jesus heals the beggar in baptism, eager and faithful discipleship is the appropriate response. The framework of this dynamic of response to grace offers the preacher chances to be both general and specific to the congregation.

The preacher might explore baptism and covenant, the psychology of response, the relationship between baptism and discipleship ideally and in reality, and the importance of whole-hearted desire for God's grace. A sermon might also link Jeremiah's prophecy of hope with the faith exhibited by one blind man, Bartimaeus. What did the blind man hope for in asking Jesus for help? How does the Gospel connect the physical healing with spiritual wholeness? What is the connection between restoration of sight and entering into the realm of God, as presented in Jeremiah and in the Gospel?

Twenty-fourth Sunday after Pentecost

Lutheran	Roman Catholic	Episcopal	Common Lectionary
Deut. 6:1-9	Deut. 6:2-6	Deut. 6:1-9	Deut. 6:1-9
Heb. 7:23-28	Heb. 7:23-28	Heb. 7:23-28	Heb. 7:23-28
Mark 12:28-34 (35-37)	Mark 12:28b-34	Mark 12:28-34	Mark 12:28b-34

EXEGETICAL INTERPRETATION

First Lesson: Deuteronomy 6:1-9.   Deuteronomy is the fifth book of the
Law, the Torah. Deuteronomy 17:18 refers to the "repeated Law," and its
name is taken from the Greek translation of that term. A complex book
in composition, it was probably written down around the eighth century
B.C.E. It is in substance "the book of the Law of Moses" (*Sefer Torat Moshe*)
referred to in 2 Kings 22:1—23:1-3.

Its form is that of Moses' last discourse to the people, in which he
recounts the history of God's mighty acts, retells the Law to the people,
gives them his deathbed admonition to obey the Law, blesses the tribes,
dies on a mountain overlooking the promised land, and is buried by the
angels on that mountain. Both its literary structure and the covenantal
substance of Moses' teaching have deep roots and close parallels in Middle
Eastern tradition.

The particular selection for today is chosen because it contains the *Shema*,
the great prayer of the Jewish tradition that looms large in today's Gospel.
Moses, the narrator, speaks first to the people about the "commandment"
(later the statutes and ordinances will be addressed). In this version of the
Law, there is one commandment, of which everything else is consequence
or elaboration.

Verses 1b-3 explore the motivation for obedience to the Law, which is
reflected in the books of Joshua, Judges, and many of the prophets. These
verses interpret God's covenantal offer to Israel as a straightforward promise:
if Israel obeys God and follows the Law, the people will be rewarded by
God; if they disobey, God will punish them. (Judges 2:11-23 interprets
the history of the conquest in this theological light.) The promises for
obedience are simple and very much this-worldly. Obedience to God will
result in a long life and material prosperity; the consequences of disobedience
are elaborated in other places (such as vv. 12-15).

Verses 4-5 are the *Shema* ("Hear," the first word of the verse), which has been taken into Jewish piety as the great prayer, to be said at every time of prayer, with or without a minyan, and finally to be uttered on the deathbed. In times of persecution and martyrdom, in death camps and in times of peace, the *Shema* is the first and last prayer of the Jewish people.

Its importance in the tradition does not, however, mean that the wording is unambiguous, however. Although in the Jewish tradition the *Shema* has become the watchword of monotheism, the Hebrew means something much more like: "The LORD is our God, the LORD alone." The *Shema* prays to Yahweh as the sole God of Israel, the divine covenant partner. The prayer, like the First Commandment, concerns itself with the people's relationship to God, not with ontological considerations or universal judgments, true as those may be.

Verses 5-9 express behavioral consequences of God's relationship to Israel. Verses 5-6 express an internal consequence—the people are to love God with total loyalty, the fullness of human capacity, heart, soul, and might, and to be always aware of God's commandments. Verses 7-9 are the external expression of God's primacy—to pass the Law on to one's children, to inform others in all circumstances about God's commands, and to let the Law be always present in one's everyday life. Verses 8 and 9 have been taken literally by many members of the Jewish community in the use of the *mezuzah* on the doorpost and the *tephillin* on the forehead and the arm at prayer.

Second Lesson: Hebrews 7:23-28. This section (which really begins with v. 20) is transitional from the comparison of Jesus' priesthood with the Levitical priesthood to the exploration of Jesus' atoning death, beginning in chapter 8. Verses 20-22 link Jesus with the eternal priesthood of Melchizedek, rather than the temporal priesthood of Aaron and his sons. Jesus is constituted priest by God's direct word and choice. Jesus is therefore a superior sort of priest and the guarantee of a better covenant. The image of guarantee (v. 22) makes Jesus the mediator figure, who is given by God to guarantee the new covenant for humanity. This note of the superior covenant will be a recurring and important theme in the epistle.

Verses 23-25 constitute a complex argument for Jesus' superiority to the old priesthood and covenant. They address the eternal priesthood of Jesus, and connect its eternal character with its salvific capacity. Jesus' priesthood is contrasted with the temporal succession of the Levitical priests, who succeeded each other in office. Jesus' eternal priesthood is identified not only with an eternal call of God, but with Jesus' own eternal nature. In the theology of Hebrews, such a term applied to Jesus is an ascription of divinity, because only God is eternal. Thus the excellence of Jesus' priesthood is rooted in his nature and relation to God.

Jesus, in contrast to the Levitical priests, remains (*menein*). To remain is to be stable and unchanging, to share in heavenly perfection. Because of its eternal character, his priesthood is absolute (*aparabaton*), a term that possesses theological, not simply legal connotations. The eternity, stability, and divinity of Jesus and his priesthood are essential to the theology of Hebrews.

Because Jesus is eternal and his priesthood consequently is eternal, his work for humanity also is eternal. Thus Jesus can offer humans a salvation which is eternal in the sense that there is no temporal limitation on what Jesus can offer, and also that the salvation allows people to participate in God's eternal spiritual realm. Jesus' offering of intercession (*entugchanein*) is not further specified in the text, and thus has become the subject of extensive debate over the centuries. Theologians have disputed the basis of Christ's intercessory role, what its character was, how his death and his intercession were related, and the connection between intercession and atonement.

Verses 26-28 are a concluding praise of Jesus as High Priest. The five descriptive words and phrases of the heavenly high priest relate to moral and priestly qualities (holy, blameless, undefiled, separated from sinners), and to the unique character of Jesus' priesthood (higher than the heavens).

Verse 27 is to the modern reader a somewhat confusing assertion that Jesus does not have to offer sacrifice daily (the work of the priests) with the sacrifice of the Day of Atonement (the high priest's task). The verse may also be understood to mean that Jesus offered sacrifice for his sins once in his own sacrificial death. It seems most likely that the author, not intimately familiar with actual first-century temple worship, wants to sound a note signaling the uniqueness of Jesus' atoning work—the theme of the next three chapters. The intention is not to draw a parallel or contrast between Jesus' intercession and the details of first-century temple worship. Verse 28 concludes the section by contrasting the weakness of the priests with the "Son perfected forever."

Gospel: Mark 12:28b-34. This story is the fourth of four tales of Jesus being tested about his teaching; in this case, however, he is not being debated by a hostile figure, but questioned by a friendly lawyer (scribe). Because the scribes are usually grouped with the Sadducees and the Pharisees as opponents of Jesus, it has been suggested that this, rather than Luke's, is the original version of the saying.

Perhaps the reason for placing this story at the end of several challenges to Jesus' authority is to show that Jesus was approved of by authorities within Judaism of his day, and spoke in words that are faithful to orthodox Judaism. It was common in Jesus' day to ask a rabbi for summaries of the

Law, and there are parallel stories to today's Gospel in contemporary Jewish lore. The closest is that told of Rabbi Hillel: A gentile inquirer came to him and asked him to utter the essence of the Law while standing on one foot. Hillel looked gently at him and said: "What you yourself hate to have done to you; do not do to another. That is the whole Law, everything else is commentary; go learn it."

Jesus' own response is to reduce the Law to two principles: love of God (Deut. 6:4-5, the *Shema*) and love of neighbor (Lev. 19:18). The formulation is not unique to Jesus. It is found in the Testament of the Twelve Patriarchs and in other places. One may inquire whether Jesus intended by his response what other rabbis, such as Hillel, would have meant, that one uses a basic interpretive principle, but follows the whole of the Law. Jesus certainly is understood in Mark as having meant something different, that if the principle is followed, then all the requirements of the Law do not have to be met, as with healing or the keeping of the Sabbath.

The complexity of the notion of love (*agape*) is undeniable, but clearly Jesus focuses on love of God and neighbor as the essence of the Law, and hence of God's self-revelation. The love of God encompasses the giving of the whole self to God (Mark changes the *Shema*'s "all your heart and soul and might" to "with all your heart and soul and mind and strength"). The love of neighbor is not the feeling of liking the neighbor, but of seeking the good of the other with same alacrity and energy as I seek my own good.

Mark presents the scribe as paraphrasing Jesus and then offering a pharisaic interpretation of his words, in which, in good prophetic style, obedience to this Law is understood as more important than the temple and the sacrificial system. Neither Jesus nor the Pharisees attacked cultic worship as such, but it was clearly subordinated to ethical considerations.

Jesus situates himself and the scribe in the context of Judaism obedient to the Law, not of rejection or cheapening of the Law. In the light of the accusations that will be made about Jesus and his faithfulness to the Law, Mark's claim of Jesus' faithfulness and its recognition by members of the religious establishment is an important one. It adds an important note of irony to the rapidly approaching rejection of Jesus by the religious authorities.

Jesus' praise of the scribe is approval of the scribe's readiness to enter God's realm, hearkening back to Jesus' original preaching—"repent and do penance, for God's realm is at hand" (1:15).

HOMILETICAL INTERPRETATION

First Lesson: Deuteronomy 6:1-9. At the heart of today's reading from Deuteronomy is the root and ground of Jewish belief and practice—the personal and covenantal relationship between God and the people. God has, Deuteronomy proclaims, chosen the people of Israel to be God's own people. How that choice affects the form of God's relationship to other nations and peoples is a question still discussed and debated in Judaism. The issue here, however, is not about other peoples or even other gods. Rather, the great confession of Israel is "Yahweh is our God; the LORD alone."

The covenant of Israel with God is at heart a personal relationship, characterized by love, fidelity, and mutual commitment. Today's reading makes that essence of Judaism utterly clear. Also, the preacher will want to remind the congregation that this most sacred and fundamental assertion of Judaism is a prayer, a confession uttered before God by Israel to Israel. Israel roots its life in a prayerful confession of its identity in a primary and formative relationship with God.

This relationship is the starting point of Jewish practice and theory, and of the whole identity of the Jewish people. One of the most moving stories to come out of the aftermath of World War II is that of a group of Jews gathered one late afternoon in one of the camps to consult with some government leaders about what ought to be done (and not done) to memorialize those who had died there. At the end of the meeting, after some moments of silence, one of the Jews, who had lost his wife, children, and parents in the camp, looked around sadly and angrily. "How can God have let this happen? How could God desert his own people and let us be killed like animals?" He began to weep, as did all the people in the room with him. Then, as the moment for the recitation of the *Shema* arrived, he looked around and began the age-old words: "Hear, O Israel: the LORD is our God, the LORD alone." The sound of weeping was replaced with the ancient words that give life and hope to Israel, even in the place where death had once seemed to triumph.

A sermon that focuses on this reading offers the opportunity to clarify common roots of Christianity with Judaism, as well as to identify differences in the New Testament and later Christian understanding of God and of our relationship with God. The preacher will want to be sure that the sermon doesn't turn into a lecture, but may find this an important time to share some information with the entire congregation, especially if there are particular issues about Jewish-Christian relations common in current community awareness. It might be a good opportunity to address directly some of the misapprehensions current in the particular congregation about Judaism, and any issues of anti-Semitism or anti-Judaism.

41

If the congregation is in a situation where there are few Jews, the sermon may need to inform people that the *Shema* is still the central Jewish prayer and confession, but that the Jewish community is not the same as it was in Jesus' day. Some Christian congregations may also profit from being reminded about our common heritage of prayer. Some may not be aware, for instance, that the Psalms, so important to Christian worship, are also still vital to Jewish worship.

Second Lesson: Hebrews 7:23-28. The priesthood of Jesus will form the primary theme for the preacher who focuses on the reading from Hebrews. The central issue is again the uniqueness of Jesus as the eternal priest. An exposition could be very helpful for many congregations, who will be unfamiliar with the entire scheme of priest and victim, and inadequate or adequate sacrifices. For liturgical traditions, the eucharistic language and devotional imagery of priest and victim offering will provide an opening to explain the significance of the relationship.

The preacher may also want to return to some of the images and hymns of Easter, which use the paschal language of the sacrificed lamb and of Jesus' free offering of himself. The eucharistic framework also may deliver the sermon from the medieval theories of atonement which stress the father/lord who seeks satisfaction for injured dignity. The eucharistic reference centers the preaching in Jesus' self-giving love that gives life to the community.

Another theme, related to this, is that as a result of the sacrifice of Jesus, victim and priest, we are enabled to enter into God's spiritual realm. The sermon might then explore how we enter into this realm. Through Jesus, we have an example to follow. The *imitatio Christi* is possible only because Jesus has shown us how to live and also invited us to live in the same way, exhibiting that same sort of self-giving love. If we live as Jesus lived, we also are living in God's spiritual realm because Jesus has led us there.

The unique priestly role of Jesus thus shows us and empowers us to live lives in a new relationship with God. Before Jesus, in the theology of Hebrews our lives were caught in a life that was subject to constant and imperfect efforts to satisfy God through sacrifices of things for our sinfulness. Because of Jesus' self-sacrifice, that new relationship is now secured for us. Our role is to live rightly in it.

Gospel: Mark 12:28b-34. Today's Gospel is best proclaimed in the light of its Hebrew Scripture antecedent (Deut. 6:4). The Gospel unquestionably is intended by Mark to present Jesus as part of the Jewish tradition, well respected and regarded by at least some of its learned representatives. The preacher may wish to take this opportunity to situate Jesus specifically in his Jewish milieu. Many Christians assume that the uniqueness of Jesus requires severing him from his own Jewish roots. Today the preacher can rectify that deep misapprehension.

It may be helpful to note that the restoration of the Hebrew Scripture reading to each liturgy is recent in the church's history; it happened in the 1960s after an absence of many centuries. The presence of this reading reemphasizes the Jewish roots of Christianity, and the reality that to Jesus and the disciples, the "Bible" was what we call the "Old Testament." The preacher can point to this liturgical development, and then connect it to the substance of today's readings, which very clearly affirm Jesus as a loyal (if critical and independent-minded) Jew, acknowledged as such by others in his tradition.

In the light of the general anti-Judaism of the historic Christian tradition, it is important for congregations from time to time to be clearly and forcefully reminded of their Jewish heritage, and of Jesus' own relationship to Judaism. Jesus is certainly unique in the Jewish tradition, but no Christian can understand her or his own faith without a firm foundation in Jesus' own Judaism.

This text also balances another equally essential aspect of Jesus' own reality that moves him beyond Judaism: He preached an agape which supersedes the Law. In this he goes beyond the Judaism of his own day, and pushes against the boundaries of Judaism with a force that eventually burst them.

Another related but different theme is the irony of this Gospel. Jesus was rejected *in spite of* his fidelity to Judaism. The scribe acknowledged the rightness of his claim based on an honest reading of the Law. Jesus' very faithfulness to the Scriptures became the cause of his rejection by the religious authorities. The contemporary preacher can identify many instances when we reject a religious vision in the name of religion precisely because it is too faithful to the Scriptures. One might use some historical examples as well as some contemporary issues—pacifism, poverty of the church as an institution (and even Christians as individuals), human equality (anti-racism and anti-sexism), and other questions that might be explored under this heading, if the preacher wants to stir up some excitement. The most productive technique for such an endeavor is to carefully and plainly marshal one's facts and observations. Good stories that force people to draw conclusions about truth and religions are highly effective.

Twenty-fifth Sunday after Pentecost

Lutheran	Roman Catholic	Episcopal	Common Lectionary
1 Kings 17:8-16	1 Kings 17:10-16	1 Kings 17:8-16	1 Kings 17:8-16
Heb. 9:24-28	Heb. 9:24-28	Heb. 9:24-28	Heb. 9:24-28
Mark 12:41-44	Mark 12:38-44 or 12:41-44	Mark 12:38-44	Mark 12:38-44

EXEGETICAL INTERPRETATION

First Lesson: 1 Kings 17:8-16. Scholars assert that Joshua, Judges, Samuel, and Kings were originally one work, a history of Israel from the conquest to the exile, and that the division into books was originally a matter of convenience. Most believe that some material may have originated before the exile. However, the primary author, animated by a Deuteronomic theological perspective, wrote the work during the first years of the Babylonian exile to warn and guide the people in remaking the nation, in hope of the return of the people to Israel.

The reading for today is part of the Elijah cycle. It appears to have been chosen because it refers to a widow, and thus echoes that theme of the Gospel. Elijah is the great prophetic exemplification of Deuteronomic theology—the raison d'être of human existence is total dedication to the one God of Israel. That this God is a jealous God is an important concept for Deuteronomic theology. When Israel follows this God faithfully, God prospers the nation in every way. However, when the people disobey God by worshiping false deities, oppressing the poor, and ignoring the Law of Moses, they will be punished by natural disasters, invasions, and finally by exile.

The Elijah story is part of a long description of the Northern Kingdom, Israel, stretching from 1 Kings 17 to 2 Kings 10. It occurs early in the Elijah saga, just after Elijah has spoken God's judgment on Ahab, that there will be a drought in the land because of his sins. Obeying God's voice, the prophet flees to Zarephath, after the wadi to which he had first gone has dried up and the ravens have ceased to bring him food. He calls on a widow he meets at the gate of the city, gathering wood for a fire.

The widow's poverty is shown by her presence at the gates gathering wood that is lying around. The prophet asks her for water, which she can provide, but she has no food to offer him. Then, just as the prophet has spoken a word of judgment to the king, he speaks one of hope to the widow. He promises that if she brings him a cake of meal, that God will miraculously sustain her supply of oil and grain until the drought is over. This element of the miraculous—bringing the drought as a sign of God's punishment, offering survival to the widow as a reward for obedience to God's prophet—dramatizes the power of Israel's God over nature in order to reward and punish obedience to the Law.

The prophet Elijah (*Eli-jah*, Yahweh is God) is the actor, the voice of the uncompromising power of Israel's God. The widow herself is at first almost invisible; there are, however, several interesting aspects to her presence in the tale. Zarephath is on the Phoenician coast; thus the city is not part of Israel, and Elijah's presence is another manifestation of Yahweh's sovereignty over the whole world, not just Israel.

The widow is not introduced as a displaced Israelite, and thus must be understood as just another inhabitant of that city. Thus her faith in obeying the word of the prophet who speaks in God's name ("For thus says the LORD, the God of Israel") is even more astonishing than if she were an Israelite. Jesus refers to the extraordinary fact of Elijah being sent to a pagan widow (Luke 4:25-26) but does not focus on the faith required of her. Nonetheless, a careful reading shows her faith and obedience presented by the author in deliberate contrast to the disobedience of the people of Israel.

Second Lesson: Hebrews 9:24-28. Today's passage comes at the end of a lengthy discussion of the ministry of the Levitical priests as contrasted with that of Jesus, the unique High Priest. In it is much detailed description of the sanctuary of the Temple and the ritual of the Day of Atonement. The author meticulously contrasts the yearly repetition of the atoning sacrifice by the high priest, and the unique sacrifice of Jesus.

The Day of Atonement typology is applied to the death of Christ (vv. 23-27) and then the theme of the uniqueness of Jesus' sacrificial death is linked with the eschatological dimension of salvation (vv. 27-28). The one efficacious sacrifice of Christ is contrasted with the many earthly and inadequate sacrifices of the Old Testament priests.

The earthly-heavenly contrast is presented here in vv. 23-24. Is a platonic distinction between heavenly original and earthly dependent archetype intended? The author seems to intend that the reader assume a correspondence between heaven and earth, as discussed in chapters 8 and 9, and that the heavenly realm, as well as the earthly, needs cleansing (v. 23). Are we to imagine a literal heavenly prototype of the Temple? Why would it need cleansing?

The consensus of modern commentators is that, through very convoluted imagery, the author of Hebrews is conveying his conviction that the consciences of humans are the "heavenly things" that need to be purified, but cannot be by the offerings of the old sacrificial system. Thus the effective sacrifice must be of a different order than the blood of goats or sheep, and must come from Christ himself.

Verses 25-27 identify the uniqueness of Christ's sacrifice cleansing the heavenly places. Verses 24-25 identify the sacrifice of Jesus with his "appear[ing] in the presence of God on our behalf." Nothing more is specified about the nature of this sacrifice other than the crucifixion of Jesus as the moment of his appearance before God, when he "removes sin by his sacrifice of himself." This appearance before God's throne is "at the end of the ages" (*sunteleia ton aionon*, v. 26). This phrase, found in Matthew's Gospel and in Jewish apocalyptic writings, expresses the common early Christian belief that the crucifixion of Jesus is *the* eschatological event.

Repudiating the thought that Jesus' sacrificial death might be infinitely repeatable not only decisively replaces the Levitical cultus with Jesus' action; it also contains within it the sense of God's powerful intervention in unique temporal events to change history and affect what has happened before and is yet to come. Jesus' sacrifice is such an event. Sin is effectively removed from humanity through this sacrifice; in the following chapters the author will discuss how people from different times are saved through this unique sacrifice.

Verses 27-28 return to the issue of the second coming. According to Hebrews, the second coming of Christ is not for judgment about sin, because that has already been dealt with in his sacrificial death for the sins of many (Isa. 53:12), that is, with all human sin. Rather, the return of Jesus is for the redemption of those who await him. The eschatology of Hebrews thus focuses on the redemptive quality of the second coming, not on judgment, which has already been given and satisfied through the first offering of Christ. (The fate of unbelievers is not addressed.)

Gospel: Mark 12:38-44. This reading is linked verbally by the reference to "widow," even though the saying in vv. 38-40 and the story in vv. 41-44 are not really parallel. Verses 38-40 form the last part of the warning against the Scribes, begun in v. 35. These verses, like other blanket condemnations in the Gospel, must be read and interpreted in context of the early Christian community's differentiation of itself from a Jewish religious structure that refused to accept it on the terms it wanted. Jesus' words were originally a scathing critique of abuses by some of his religious colleagues, not a blanket allegation about the beliefs or behavior of all the scholars in Judea.

Verses 38-39 mock the self-importance of scribes who insist on recognition of their special status. The long robe is the *tallit,* worn for prayer and study, which had become a status symbol that some of the scribes wore all the time. The salutation is to be given by the less learned to the more scholarly. In the synagogue, seats on the bench below the Ark, facing the people, were at this time being given to the leadership of the religious community. Precedence in seating at banquets was highly valued, and in Jesus' time it was according to achievement in learning.

Verse 40 condemns the widespread abuse in all religious communities of a male leadership befriending widows, and extracting money from them in exchange for spiritual support. Jesus condemns this practice most heartily; his vehement words find their parallel in Pharisaic writings.

Verses 41-44 praise the generosity of the widow. The story is set in context of Jesus' teaching in the Temple (v. 35); it is very hard to know from the description in v. 41 what is meant by "the treasury." There were some thirteen receptacles for offerings around the court of the women, according to the Mishnah; perhaps Jesus is to be understood as sitting near one of them.

Because this detail is unclear, and because Jesus had no way to know that the woman had put in all she had, several commentators suggest that originally this was not a story about Jesus, but one that he told about a widow and her offering. There are a number of comparable stories from Jewish and pagan sources, so it seems quite plausible to assume that originally Jesus was telling the disciples about a poor widow.

In its present context, the story not only forms a stark and dramatic contrast with the greed and ambition of the scribes, but it introduces the theme of Jesus' self-sacrifice in his gift of his own life for humanity. Chapter 13, following immediately on it, foretells the destruction of Jerusalem and the end of the age; chapters 14 and 15 tell the passion story.

All of the details contrast the values of this world and those of God. The widow has no earthly status or power; the rich certainly do. Their contributions are indicated as great sums; the widow puts in two *lepta,* about 1/64 of a laborer's daily wage.

It is straining credulity to take all of this literally. Jesus' story is intended to underscore the heart of Jesus' moral teaching, that God looks to the disposition of the heart, the intention of giving all to God, rather than counting the amount given. The widow's negligible sum is worth more to God than the gifts of the rich, so well regarded in religious society of their day. Her gift comes from her heart and from great sacrifice; the rich offer only what they can spare easily.

HOMILETICAL INTERPRETATION

First Lesson: 1 Kings 17:8-16. This marvelously vivid story is linked with the Gospel through the theme of the faith of the widow. But because the three readings for today are so different the preacher will need to decide on which one of the readings he or she wishes to preach. If the Elijah story is the focus, there are several enticing choices.

One possibility is to offer a mini-lecture on Deuteronomic theology. Of course, one would not phrase one's intentions so bluntly, but one might begin by speaking of the intense faith of the prophet Elijah and his significance for Israel. Elijah lived and preached a very strong and specific doctrine about God and God's relationship to the nation. He ran afoul of the king because his beliefs were strong and the king was quite opposed to him. The enduring influence of Elijah's vision shaped the whole religion of Israel. Thus, we might conclude in our introduction, it is very important for us, as spiritual descendants of the people of Israel, to know Elijah's beliefs.

We then might offer a description of Elijah's theology, with its insistence that God is a jealous God, that God expects people to obey the covenant, and that God will reward those who do and punish those who don't. The preacher may also then include a discussion of American popular religion as it was formed by Deuteronomic theology. The sermon may then address the ways in which this theology is tested by events, and how it holds up in the Scriptures and in real life. Elijah's life can offer some insights into strengths and weaknesses of this interpretation of God's involvement in our history that the preacher may want to suggest with respect to current events.

Another obvious theme connected with the Elijah cycle is the faith of the prophet, who leaves his own land of Israel to flee to Zarephath during the drought. He has no connections and, as a foreigner, can scarcely expect to be welcomed in a place also affected by the severe drought. Yet he responded immediately to God's message to go to the city, exhibiting in his own person the absolute faith in God to which he was recalling Israel.

A related theme, suggested by the faith of the widow in the Gospel, is the widow in this story of Elijah. The preacher can paint vivid word pictures of the widow in her poverty, gathering sticks by the city gates. She is not a Jew, and probably has no idea who the God of Israel is. Instead, in a city affected by food shortages, she prepares for death by starvation, disappointed by her gods.

Suddenly, into her life bursts the blunt, confident Elijah, who tells her what she is to do in obedience to the commandments of her God. Why does she respond to this servant of a God she does not worship? Is she ready to grasp at straws? Does she not care anymore? Has a spark of faith been struck in her heart? Although the preacher ought to resist the temptation to read into the Scriptures what is not there, the widow does in fact act on faith, and becomes an example of faith in Elijah's life story.

Because Israel's God is not known to her, she becomes an exemplar of faith, in contrast to Israel. Her story becomes an opportunity to explore the strength of faith that is not so strong and clear as Elijah's, but that rises to challenges and is willing to follow God even into the unknown.

Second Lesson: Hebrews 9:24-28. Most non-Jews know about the Day of Atonement, Yom Kippur. A very helpful sermon for most congregations would be a simple explanation of the temple observance of the Day of Atonement, today's observance of the Day, and what Jews understand Yom Kippur to be. In this context one can then place the uniqueness of Jesus' sacrificial death. Because the focus in this reading is on the role of the high priest, special attention should be paid to the sacrificial character of the temple observance, as contrasted with the necessarily internalized synagogue worship.

In the perspective of the Jewish background, Jesus' uniqueness must be explored with regard both to his priestly role and to his character as a sacrifice for atonement. For fullest effect, the sermon will distinguish those roles and make them explicit for the congregation. It may also be helpful to make the liturgical dimensions of atonement quite clear as they are presented in the Hebrew Scriptures.

In this passage, particularly, the uniqueness of Jesus that cleanses humans from sin is contrasted with the sacrifices of the Law. This cleansing is internal, not external. The sacrifices of the old Law made people ritually clean and in that sense worthy to enter into the temple, the earthly sanctuary. However, the cleansing really needed is internal, of the conscience. That is the cleansing which only Jesus is able to do, because he can reach both God and humanity internally, being in himself both "the reflection of God's very being" and also "like us in all things except sin." Only Jesus can be effective priest and victim, and thus also the only effective agent of atonement. This is heavy theology, but could be a good direction for a congregation that wants or needs to wrestle openly with its Christology.

This passage (v. 28) also presents an eschatology that is not apocalyptic, and may be very attractive to many people. The author asserts that the second coming of Jesus is "not to deal with sin but to save those who are waiting for him." Hebrews knows no "day of doom." Jesus' second coming, no matter how one might interpret it, is perceived as only for the believers' benefit and comfort. (Hebrews doesn't even raise the question of universal judgment.) Jesus' glorious second coming into the world is redemptive.

This thought of course raises the whole issue of judgment, eschatology, and human redemption. It might thus be a good opportunity to prepare people for Advent, and to face squarely most modern Christians' difficulties with the whole notion of eschatology (not only apocalypse).

Gospel: Mark 12:38-44. The Gospel for today is difficult to preach about as a unity because two different types of narrative are put together with the mere verbal link of the word "widow." The first story is a caricature of the scribes' abuse of power. A brave preacher might tackle this headlong, and put Jesus' two-thousand-year-old condemnation into contemporary language and figures. Because it is a direct assault on the religious establishment, and to some extent on Jesus' peers, translating it into contemporary language is quite difficult without sounding self-righteous or as though one is trying to play to the gallery at colleagues' expense.

Instead, one might well try to tackle the self-righteous behavior of all of us. Certainly one can find more than enough examples in any congregation. Even if the rebuke stings, humor and the sense that everyone is included among the guilty enable most members of the congregation to hear words which, like any good satire, call us to reform.

The story of the widow's mite is so well known as to invite maudlin sentimentality in preaching about it. Instead, the preacher may well decide to use the story as Mark does, to contrast the greed and ambition of the scribes with the poor widow. One can find ample sermonic material for this theme. The controlling behavior of the powerful of both church and state can be painfully abusive for the health of the community, whereas the generosity of the poor, who do not press self-important claims, enriches the entire community.

The preacher may also analyze from this perspective the contemporary stewardship scene, in which proportionate giving is much higher among the poor than the well-to-do. The question, then, is how people actually can and will change in conformity with the spirit of the poor widow rather than the prosperous and self-important scribes.

The Gospel's own structure suggests to the preacher that the self-sacrifice of the widow be viewed as a kind of anticipation of Jesus' own self-sacrifice to come in Jerusalem. The gift of the widow seems extravagant; the context connects to Jesus' own gift of love to the world. The homiletic movement of the story can thus direct the congregation toward the deep feelings of the heart that give rise to the most profound and generous gifts to others. The root is always love of God, because only the lover of God is free to give without counting the cost.

Twenty-sixth Sunday after Pentecost

Lutheran	Roman Catholic	Episcopal	Common Lectionary
Dan. 12:1-3	Dan. 12:1-3	Dan. 12:1-4a (5-13)	Dan. 7:9-14
Heb. 10:11-18	Heb. 10:11-14, 18	Heb. 10:31-39	Heb. 10:11-18
Mark 13:1-13	Mark 13:24-32	Mark 13:14-23	Mark 13:24-32

EXEGETICAL INTERPRETATION

First Lesson: Daniel 7:9-14; 12:1-3. The book of Daniel, selected because of references to it in today's Gospel, falls into two obvious divisions: Daniel A, chapters 1–6, stories about the prophetic and judicial activity of Daniel; Daniel B, chapters 7–12, a series of revelations given to the prophet. The author of the Book of Daniel claims to be writing around the last year of the Babylonian Age and beginning of the Persian Age, around 545–535 B.C.E. Internal evidence, however, suggests a far more complex dating, with Daniel B dating from the reign of Antiochus IV, about 168–165 B.C.E.

Daniel's literary form is that of an apocalypse, the interpretation of contemporary events in the light of an immanently expected intervention of God to put to rights the intolerable evil. The apocalyptic author perceives the world as being in so catastrophic a situation that only God can set it to rights again. God's intervention is sudden and unexpected by human beings, although certain signs are given by God to allow the faithful to prepare themselves for God's overpowering advent.

The Daniel of B is not the wise counselor or judge, as in Daniel A, but an apocalyptic seer. The theological problem he confronts is, Why ought the people of Israel to be faithful to the covenant in light of the exile and now the present intense persecutions by rulers who favor a rationalist, Greek culture? The response of Daniel is that God's faithful love will bring about a new age, overcoming even the extreme violence and degradations brought upon the people by God's enemies.

In chapter 7 is found the vision of the passing of the four earthly kingdoms to make room for the heavenly kingdom. The scene is that of the heavenly court, where God (the "Ancient One" of Ps. 90:2) is seated on his throne (Ez. 1:15-26), surrounded by innumerable attendants (v. 10). God's judgment is effective, and is able to destroy one beast; the others live only at

51

God's sufferance. The apocalyptic genre frequently describes God's immediate and direct intervention in history in fabulous language about monsters and mysterious beings.

The one like a human being (son of man) in v. 13 comes with the accompaniments of a heavenly being, the "clouds of heaven." The designation of "like a human being" suggests one truly made in the image of God (Gen. 1:26), fulfilling God's intentions for humanity. He and his dominion, in contrast to the earthly rulers, disobedient to God, will last eternally. Thus he shares in some way the divinity of the Ancient One, because he is given an everlasting dominion, and is to be served by all people.

Chapters 11–12 are said to be from the third year of King Cyrus of Persia. Daniel, who has prayed to God to know the future, receives a "word" from an angel. The prophecies bring the author down to the present time (the reign of Antiochus IV, persecutor of the Jews) and predict what will happen after that. Chapter 12 foretells the growth of the persecution (the "time of anguish"), the resurrection of the dead to judgment, the divine purification, and restoration of the world.

After the (historically unfulfilled) predictions of the destruction of Antiochus, Dan. 12:1-4 offers the hidden (v. 4) knowledge about the end time. Michael is the angelic prince appointed to watch over the people in their final trial. A time of unique and unsurpassed anguish and suffering is predicted for the people, in language with many parallels in other apocalyptic literature. The deliverance from this period of anguish is found in the inauguration of a new age, heralded by the resurrection of the dead. This mention of a resurrection to reward or punishment is the first clear mention of resurrection in the Bible.

Second Lesson: Hebrews 10:11-18. These verses of Hebrews mark the ending of the theological exposition of the sacrifice of Jesus for humanity; they offer a resumé of the fundamental themes of the uniqueness and efficacious character of human redemption through Jesus' sacrifice of himself. It contrasts the many, repetitive, and ineffective sacrifices of the old priesthood with the one eternally effective sacrifice of Jesus. In vv. 12-13, Jesus' enthronement and eternal priesthood, following his sacrifice, are described with the language of Psalm 110, previously used in 7:17, 21. An eschatological dimension is added through the use of the Jeremiah 31:33-34 passage, which heralds the themes of the upcoming chapters.

Verse 11 contrasts "every priest" (in this sense including the high priest) of the old Law, who stands before the altar making constant but inadequate intercession, with Christ. Christ offers one sacrifice and sits, in the posture of a king ruling. The antithesis between the many sacrifices of the old

Law and the one sacrifice of Jesus is insisted upon again. Jesus is described, with the messianic language of Psalm 110, as one seated on God's right hand, a familiar theme in early Christian theology, and an obvious contrast with the priests of the old covenant standing in attendance at the altar.

The phrase "for all time" (*eis to diēnekes*) seems to be used with deliberate ambiguity to include the perpetual effects of Christ's sacrifice and also his enthronement for all time. That same phrase used in v. 12 is also used in v. 14 to refer directly to the sanctification of all those perfected by Jesus' sacrifice.

Verse 13 continues the use of Psalm 110 to articulate the theme of eschatological subjection of Jesus' enemies. Because Jesus' sacrifice is effective, the present time is thus a time of waiting for the effects of Jesus' victory to be fully realized in the world. Verse 14 points again to the single offering (with an implied contrast to the many sacrifices of the old covenant) through which Christ has perfected those who are sanctified. The one sacrifice has perfected those who are even now being made holy. Thus the one act with eternal consequences is in the present being appropriated by believers. Verse 14 suggests the appropriation of redemption still being worked out among Christ's followers.

The quotation from Jeremiah (31:33-34) in verses 16-18 is slightly reworded (nothing unusual in light of the looser style of quotation in any ancient work). Dropping the explicit reference to the people of Israel, the author of Hebrews refers simply to "them" and draws together the promise to write the new law on their hearts with the promise to forgive sins permanently. Thus the theme of the preceding christological verses is applied to the believers, who enter into a new, inward relationship with God through the priestly intercession of Jesus and his glorification in the new kingdom.

The Episcopal Lectionary departs from this order and uses Heb. 10:31-39. This section treats the struggles experienced by the persecuted followers of Jesus, and the reward that they will receive because of the persistence of their faith. This reading harmonizes with the theme in the Gospel reading of the persecution of the faithful during the upheavals of the last times.

Gospel: Mark 13:24-32. The various lectionaries all use Mark 13, but each uses a slightly different passage: Lutheran, 1-13; Roman Catholic, 24-32; Episcopal, 14-23; Common, 24-32. In Mark this chapter is presented as the culmination of Jesus' teachings. A twentieth-century Christian, or even one from the age of the Gospel of John, would almost certainly not have chosen this collection of apocalyptic predictions to be Jesus' last discourse; Mark, however, finds it most appropriate. Because the essential material of the passion account of chapters 14 and 15 was already in existence, we may regard this choice as a clear statement of the Gospel writer's judgment of the culmination of Jesus' teaching.

The chapter combines characteristics of the apocalyptic genre with the last discourse of a dying leader (parallels in Genesis 48–49; Deuteronomy 31–32; Joshua 23–24; 1 Samuel 12; 1 Chronicles 28–29). Sometimes this chapter is called the "little apocalypse." It is generally regarded as containing some genuine sayings of Jesus, as well as expansions made to confront later developments, such as the actual destruction of the temple.

The setting of the chapter is just outside the temple precincts, taking place after Jesus has left the temple proper, perhaps going into the Kidron Valley. One could see from there the huge foundation stones and the impressive construction of the temple. An anonymous disciple makes an admiring remark about the temple, and here and in a parallel saying to Matt. 24:1-3 and Luke 21:5-7, Jesus responds with a prediction that the temple will be destroyed, and "not one stone will be left upon another; all will be destroyed."

The apocalyptic material begins when Jesus has reached the Mount of Olives, and the four disciples closest to Jesus (Peter, James, John, and Andrew) approach him and ask him to make plain to them when and how these hidden things will happen. Then Jesus begins to teach them, following a convention in the Gospel of Mark, that Jesus teaches some or all of the disciples privately in order to clear up difficulties or misunderstandings in his public teaching. Usually it is these four, who then provide leadership to the others.

The discourse is divided into four sections: vv. 5-13, the miseries preceding the last days; vv. 14-23, an account of the last days; vv. 24-27, the return of the "Son of Man"; vv. 28-38, related sayings of Jesus that give perspective to this prediction of the end times. The section chosen by the Common Lectionary (24-32) includes some of the material about the end time and most of the other sayings in the chapter.

The cosmic details in vv. 24-25 refer to a general disintegration of the order in the natural world. Verse 26 refers to Dan. 7:13 and the coming of the heavenly one who is like a human being. Verse 27 portrays the angels as messianic agents, gathering the elect; in Jewish apocalyptic the angels gather the Diaspora back to the Holy Land.

Verses 28-32 are of a different sort and in some ways even contradictory to the preceding treatment of the end time; they warn the disciples to see these disruptions as signs of a fulfillment that God the Father—not the Son or angels—works. The time of this end cannot be predicted by anyone. Thus we seem to have in the Gospel pericope two different eschatological traditions equally attributed to Jesus. Because the assertion attributed to

Jesus in v. 32 is also assigned to Jesus in the other Synoptics, many contemporary commentators believe this to be his own attitude (and perhaps even his direct answer to a question about the end time posed to him). This moral insistence to be ready always for the end of time is unquestionably at the core of Jesus' teaching about the coming of the reign of God.

HOMILETICAL INTERPRETATION

First Lesson: Daniel 7:9-14. In the Roman Missal the readings for the last Sunday before Advent were parallel in theme to the readings for this Sunday; they spoke of God's intervention in history and of Jesus' second coming. Thus the themes of this Sunday made a "little Advent" and a bridge from the time after Pentecost to the new liturgical year and the season of Advent. The contemporary arrangement in all the Western liturgical churches places the "apocalyptic" Sunday the second Sunday before Advent; next Sunday is the feast of Christ the King.

In fact, both of these Sundays celebrate Jesus' sovereignty. Perhaps this Sunday may be the time the preacher wishes to address that issue; one may also wait until next Sunday. The issue will be there; all the readings point to it. Two related questions almost certainly must be faced in contemporary congregations, if not directly addressed by the preacher. The first is the very notion of the sovereignty of Christ (or even of God); the second is that of the masculine imagery used to convey that sovereignty.

Because next Sunday so overtly uses the image of "king," the question of masculine language ought to be addressed in that section. Today's reading is overtly about God's sovereignty over the history of the world. The basic premise of apocalyptic writing is that God is sovereign, and the powers of evil may wreak great havoc, but will not ultimately triumph over God's good purpose for creation.

The preacher needs, sometime during the year, to confront honestly the profundity of human doubt that God is really in charge of the world. In contemporary Western culture, that doubt will take at least two basic forms. One is the heartfelt response to all the misery in the world. How could a good God be responsible for the horror and chaos we see around us? If the world is such a mess, with no good God intervening, no one is in charge. There is no sovereign God for us humans. Two thousand years of theology have wrestled with that perception, and the preacher will need such theological help to illumine the possible responses for the congregation.

Today, however, the concept of God's sovereignty is being questioned critically. There *ought* to be no sovereign God, the critics assert. If humans are to be mature, they are responsible for their own decisions, and not to be "lorded over," even by God. One version of this position ignores ontological claims, and insists that a good God would not relate to us as a sovereign, but as friend and companion. All of the biblical material relating to God's sovereignty is therefore to be ignored or rejected, they suggest, and only that which expresses God's respect for humans as companions, co-creators, and in a real sense as equal participants in the unfolding of life is to be accepted.

The preacher who sees the need to tackle this theme in a particular congregation will want to carefully study the particular form of the questioning of the notion of sovereignty of God. One approach, which can be used directly or indirectly, is to draw from the reading what sort of sovereignty God exercises. One particular aspect of the Daniel reading is especially useful for that approach.

The "Son of Man" or "the one like a human being" refers back to the creation story in Genesis 1–2. This messianic figure is a glorified and idealized human being, one who is what human beings ought to be. This one is given by the Ancient of Days, the God figure, sovereignty over the earth and all its peoples. Thus one can read into the text that God is not sovereign over humanity to oppress us, but to lead us to the fullest freedom of which we are capable. "The one like a human being" is the messianic ruler because humanity living up to its vocation to be fully in God's image is given the power by God to rule over itself. God's sovereignty is not foreign and imposed on us, but respects us and guides to true maturity our own nature.

Such an approach is not the end point of such theological explorations of sovereignty, but seems a good beginning for many congregations. A positive exploration of God's sovereignty can thus be of benefit and interest to those enmeshed in the debate, as well as those for whom it is not now a question.

Second Lesson: Hebrews 10:11-18. Much of today's reading is a recapitulation of the theme of the unique ministry of Jesus. This repetitiousness can be especially helpful to the preacher if one has not preached much or at all about Hebrews, and chooses to begin now.

Jesus' sovereignty in the "time between the times" is graphically portrayed in language reminiscent of Psalm 2 and of the Acts of the Apostles. Jesus, who has performed his unique sacrifice of himself, is seated as a glorified ruler at God's right hand, waiting for his triumph over his enemies. Thus, Jesus' role is not active intervention, but being present in the process of sanctification of the community of the redeemed. Jesus' sovereignty lies in the community's appropriation of what already is theirs through Jesus' high priestly work.

Thus in this time before the end of time, the drama is internal. The prophecy of Jeremiah offers the preacher the opportunity to stress the internal dynamics of the sovereignty of Jesus. The "rule" is not in making us do something, but in the process of conversion, by which people respond to God's invitation and accept as their own the covenant with God. This conversion is not to a new set of duties or even loyalties, but the transformation into people who *want* to live as God's people. For most preachers, the operative word for the sermon will be *want*, because it changes the substance of divine sovereignty and even of sanctification into a voluntary and pleasurable human possibility.

Gospel: Mark 13:24-32. The form of this Gospel story offers the preacher an entrée in explaining apocalyptic that comes directly from the Gospel itself. The first part of the story is in verses 1-2 of this chapter, when Jesus prophesies the destruction of the temple. The verses that follow recount Jesus' "secret" teaching to Peter, James, John, and Andrew as they look at the temple from the Mount of Olives.

By taking the disciples' inquiry in verse 3, the preacher can lead the congregation into a sympathetic understanding of apocalyptic literature. In effect, the disciples ask, "The present human situation looks so iniquitous, and we cannot see how God can untangle the web. How are we to try to understand God's intentions for the world?" Apocalypse is the human effort to explain what God will do to put things right. It is "hidden" because only the elect have the faith to accept God's assurance and thus to understand.

Another dimension of this story which a congregation may find helpful is that Jesus explains the hidden purposes of God to leaders in the community of the apostles. This scheme of Jesus' instruction of leaders can be used to explore the role of the congregation in their own listening to God in the Scriptures, worship of the church, and their personal prayer and study. As they listen to Jesus, as baptized Christians they are charged to go forth and make the hidden clear. As Jesus worked through the disciples, Jesus works through people today.

Verses 28-32 probably represent Jesus' own perspective on the end of time, and are of vital importance. The implication of not knowing the day or the hour of the end of time is essential to the Christian faith, because it requires an attitude of constant readiness. The preacher may find it helpful to connect the theme of readiness to that of our living in a time of crisis. If we are to be in a state of constant readiness, all of our life must be lived as though God's judgment will come any minute. There are any number of ways of exploring various aspects of constant human readiness for God's presence; the preacher may wish to concentrate on one or to identify several but with less thorough consideration.

Christ the King
Last Sunday after Pentecost

Lutheran	Roman Catholic	Episcopal	Common Lectionary
Dan. 7:13-14	Dan. 7:13-14	Dan. 7:9-14	Jer. 23:1-6
Rev. 1:4b-8	Rev. 1:5-8	Rev. 1:1-8	Rev. 1:4b-8
John 18:33-37	John 18:33b-37	John 18:33-37 or Mark 11:1-11	John 18:33-37

EXEGETICAL INTERPRETATION

First Lesson: Jeremiah 23:1-6. In the Roman Catholic and Lutheran calendars this last Sunday after Pentecost is entitled the Feast of Christ the King; although the Episcopal Church calendar does not use the title, the collect and readings share the theme of Jesus' divine sovereignty. The Common Lectionary uses Jer. 23:1-6; Episcopal, Lutheran, and Roman Catholic Lectionaries use Dan. 7:13-14, which was treated in last week's readings. The section of the prophet Jeremiah used in the Common Lectionary originated in a very early period of Israel's development of its messianic theology. Probably it dates from a time just after the reign of King Zedekiah (596–586 B.C.E.).

Zedekiah was placed on the throne of Judah as a subordinate ruler after the first Babylonian conquest by Nebuchadnezzar. When, despite the prophet's warnings, the king led a new rebellion against the Babylonians, they recaptured Jerusalem, sacked the city, and took the king and the notables of the city into exile in Babylon. Because Zedekiah was the last lineal descendant of David, his deposition and exile occasioned a new crisis for the Jewish community about the nature of God's divinely promised kingship for the covenant people.

Verses 1-2 offer God's reproach to the kings of Israel who have been unworthy shepherds. The shepherd image for the king has deep roots in Middle Eastern pastoral culture; it also reminds the hearers of King David, the shepherd and exemplar of the just king. Ezekiel 34 contains the strongest prophetic condemnation of the kings as bad shepherds, and the prophet Jeremiah articulates the same criticism of the shepherds (by implication the political and religious leaders) who neglect the flock, whose actions even scatter the flock.

In verses 2-4, in the face of the terrible doom that the prophet anticipates for the people as they are scattered and lost by the shepherds who do evil, he also foresees a restoration for good. The people are God's people (vv. 1, 3) and God will not let them be destroyed by the evil shepherds. God promises to bring the "remnant of my flock" back from exile (v. 3). There is no developed theology of the righteous remnant here, or any moral prediction or vision of a cosmic or eschatological future for the people.

God will rescue the people from their evil fate, the exiles will return from Babylon, and better times are ahead for them. That seems to be what the prophet predicts in the name of the messianic shepherd. The people of God will be cared for, and they will prosper, because God's promises to the people will be fulfilled.

The shepherd is connected with the Davidic descendent in v. 5; the prophet foresees the restoration of David's line to provide a "righteous branch" (*semah*), who will behave as a good king ought, not as the evil shepherds have done. The behavior described follows the model laid down for the ideal king (e.g., Psalm 72) who cares for the people, doing God's justice on the earth, being a good shepherd and king.

Verse 6 describes the effects of the good king's reign on the land: Judah will be saved and Israel will live in safety. The messianic king is thus foreseen to be God's king for the whole of the nation, for a reunited nation, not just Israel or Judah. The prophet interprets the separation of the two nations as an evil which will be overcome by the messianic king who inaugurates the restoration God wills. The name of the new king is "the Lord is my righteousness," almost a play on the name of King Zedekiah ("Yahweh is righteousness"), as though to say that God will raise up a Davidic king to fulfill the promise of Zedekiah's name.

Second Lesson: Revelation 1:4b-8. The Book of Revelation is a highly complex work, which even in the early church was regarded as difficult to interpret. Consequently, the book was late in being admitted into the canon. Revelation (Apocalypse) is of that genre of works which purports to interpret a highly complicated system of visions and signs in order to disclose secrets about God's ending of the world's time and the establishment of the new age. The author is John, perhaps a Palestinian Jew living in Asia Minor during the later part of the first century. Revelation is filled with imagery, both directly used and also sometimes significantly changed, from the Hebrew Scriptures.

Immediately after the prologue (vv. 1-3), John salutes the seven representative Asian churches to whom the book is addressed. Perhaps John exercised some sort of oversight over the churches of the Roman province of Asia. His knowledge of and concern for them seems to far exceed the concern of one who is simply a brother (v. 9). There were, of course, many more churches than the seven he addresses in v. 4, but seven is the number of completeness, and will be so used in other places in Revelation. Thus, these churches are representative of all the churches. Probably John intended us to be reminded of Zechariah 4, and the image of Israel as a sevenfold candelabra, with the seven lamps.

"Grace and peace" is a Christian greeting heard also in the epistles of Paul. "From him who was and is and is to come" is an expansion of the name of God given to Moses in the Book of Exodus. The seven spirits before the throne are probably the seven archangels of late Jewish angelology, but it may also refer to the sevenfold Spirit of God (Isa. 11:2).

Jesus Christ is presented as also before God's throne, introduced by titles that emphasize his relationship to persecuted Christians: "faithful witness, firstborn from the dead, and the ruler of the kings of the earth." *Faithful witness* to those who have borne witness with their lives, *first born from the dead* as the one who offers life to them in God's name and is head of the church, *and the ruler of the kings of earth* as the heavenly power to whom even the might of the Roman Empire must bow.

Verses 5-6 follow the epistolary form by a prayerful address to Christ. His love is testified to as eternal and present; his redemption is a unique act already accomplished for humanity; its effect is to establish a dominion in which the people of the Christian community are priests to serve God (Exod. 19:6). In Rev. 2:26, John will add that this priestly dominion, as a sharing in Christ's messianic reign, also gives God's people royal authority over the nations that will be exercised in the end time.

In vv. 7-8 John describes the parousia, using the imagery of Dan. 7:13 and Zech. 12:10—13:1. Matthew 24:30 uses the same combination of images, so it seems likely that it was a popular approach in the early church. Verse 7 asserts that the nations will see the crucified Christ returning, glorified in the clouds, and that all, including those who pierced him, will lament on his account. This certainly suggests something like the penitential grief of Zechariah, although it does not necessarily mean true repentance.

In v. 8, Alpha and Omega, the beginning and end, suggesting time and history as well as creative intention, is spoken by God as a self-identification. John adds, as God's name, the "I am" as spoken in v. 4:b, adding that this God is the almighty, the *pantocrator* (an LXX translation of *Yahweh Sabbaoth*). Thus John connects God's creative might with redemptive love.

Gospel: John 18:33-37. Choice is one of the most consistent themes in John's Gospel. Those who meet Jesus must choose: Who do they think Jesus is, and what does he mean for the course of their lives? From the prologue to the resurrection, Jesus constantly confronts people with the necessity of choosing, of judging themselves in the light of God's will for the world. In the story of the passion and death of Jesus, John holds up for us the human participation shaping the tragic story of Jesus' suffering and death.

Pilate and Jesus are the chief actors in today's Gospel reading. The setting is inside the Praetorium, after Jesus has been arrested by the temple soldiers and handed over to Pilate for trial. Reflecting a late first-century world in which the synagogue had grown increasingly hostile to the growing movement of Jesus' followers, the early Christians, adapting to the gentile world, sought to minimize Roman responsibility for Jesus' execution. Pilate, the representative of Roman authority, appears to be caught between Jewish demands for Jesus' death and Roman justice, which could acquit him. As the story begins, Pilate, showing a sensitivity utterly lacking in the other historical records of him, summons Jesus to ask him: "Are you King of the Jews?" (v. 33)

Thus Pilate's question reveals his concern—the intersection of Jesus' ministry with Roman political authority. Jesus has been accused of violating Roman law and order, and Pilate seeks to discover if he is a political rebel, or a religious figure who can safely be released.

Verses 34-35 offer an exchange of questions, as Jesus asks how Pilate has learned that Jesus is a king, and Pilate asks what he has done to be handed over by his own people. This question sets up a situation in which one might expect Pilate to release Jesus as not guilty by Roman law. In John's eyes, Pilate's tragedy is that he has asked the questions to discover truth, and has received a response, but he refuses the redemptive truth offered him by Jesus.

Jesus repudiates the power of his dominion (*basileia*) as being that of this world; it does not come from this political order. Jesus adduces the disciples' unwillingness to fight to deliver him as proof of the unworldliness of Jesus' power. Although this ought to have proven to Pilate Jesus' innocence, he pursues the issue of Jesus' kingship. Jesus' response, "You say that I am," is not an affirmation, but an assertion that to deny the statement would be false but to affirm it would not be really true either.

Thus Jesus clarifies his kingship as "to testify to the truth." (One should note that Jesus speaks here of his exercise of kingship, not the extent of the kingdom, *basileia tou Theou*.) His form of sovereignty is to testify to God's redemptive truth (John 14:6). Jesus' kingship is that of the Good Shepherd (John 10:3, 16-18), who calls the sheep to life.

But Pilate, on hearing Jesus' invitation that also demands that he choose to listen to Jesus' voice, refuses his offer, throwing back to Jesus his cynical refusal: "What is truth?" In John's Gospel, where Jesus is clearly identified as God's truth made flesh for us as far back as the prologue (1:14), this tragic scene represents not only Pilate's own personal refusal, but a repudiation of Jesus on behalf of the gentile world as definitive as that of the religious authorities and the people of Israel.

HOMILETICAL INTERPRETATION

First Lesson: Jeremiah 23:1-6. In last week's reading, under the discussion of the Hebrew Scripture we examined one aspect of the contemporary discussion about God's sovereignty. Today's reading brings up other topics that also are not explicit issues in all congregations, but about which the preacher must be prepared to preach.

Particularly among feminists, the masculine language of the biblical images for God as sovereign are in and of themselves off-putting, if not also sufficient to lead to the rejection of all language about God's sovereignty. Such wording is understood to articulate and thus sanctify with divine blessing a patriarchal domination by which women are either oppressed or patronized in dependent relationships. To call God *king* or *shepherd* is to sanctify these male power relationships for Christians. If the Bible really means that these terms are sacred and must be retained, then, according to many feminists, the Bible must be rejected; if these terms can be understood as signs and interpreted in a nonsexist framework, then nonsexist, nonpatriarchal language must be used instead of the old terms.

From quite another perspective, many members of minority communities have insisted that because the male power structures are experienced as so oppressive, to affirm God as *the* king and *the* shepherd is to deabsolutize all human power and to ascribe sovereignty to God alone. This move is perceived as liberating for male and female humans alike, especially because the scriptural images of God refer to a divine reality that both includes and far transcends all masculine and feminine references. (This interpretation certainly returns to the spirit of the early Christians' cry, "Jesus is Lord," a statement that withdrew from the emperor and states all claims to divinity and to absolute loyalty from any human person.)

In a sermon, the most effective approach seems to be to acknowledge the objections, examine the historical context of the images and references in the Scripture, and explore how to interpret them historically and theologically. The most crucial principles for a contemporary Christian would include an acknowledgment that the movement of the Scripture is toward a God who is neither male nor female, but was revealed in a world whose social structure used predominantly male imagery with some female language and images.

One would also include in a sermon the scriptural insistence that God's grace moves people to freedom in Christ. This concern is balanced by the need to be faithful to the intention, if not the precise wording of the Scripture. That idea is tricky, but indispensable for the preacher. Examples might be used, for instance, with language about "kingdom" or "warrior." In homiletical response to the various questions about the patriarchal and male language of Scripture, the preacher may want to focus on helping people interpret and use the Scriptures to discover a meaning that is not frozen in time two or three thousand years ago. The other obvious approach is indirect, to explore precisely what is said about shepherding and kingship in the Scriptures. Certainly in these passages (and almost inevitably in the Scriptures), the model offered, even in its most male-dominated form, is contrary to the ideals of a patriarchal society, and any notion of domination or exploitation under any circumstances.

Specifically in this passage, an ideal of shepherding and kingship is upheld that focuses on the shepherd as nurturer and guardian. Exploitive shepherds are condemned, and God promises the people good shepherds and kings. Because this passage is not usually linked in people's minds with the New Testament good shepherd figure, one can explore with fewer preconceptions the ideal of leadership described here.

Second Lesson: Revelation 1:4b-8. The reading comprises both the greeting and the address to Jesus. The "grace and peace" greeting was apparently a common greeting in the early Christian community, and the preacher may wish to ask the congregation what grace and peace we wish for each other. Some considerable exploration can be done, both of the biblical meaning and of contemporary understandings of grace and peace. What does this initial greeting express about the identity and ideals of the Christian community? What do our own greetings and first comments to people suggest about our own operative values? (What's your name? Where do you live? Are you married? What do you do for a living?)

The greeting in Revelation is also, the preacher will note, from God. What does the greeting, which is linked with God's name, reveal about God's character and will for humanity? Because in this context God's name is God's self-introduction to humanity, what sort of God does John show us in Revelation? The titles offer a complex, probably trinitarian greeting, which expresses a rich theology of God's self-disclosure to the churches that are addressed.

The invocation of Christ that follows the greeting encompasses a description of God active in human history from beginning to end, *Alpha* and *Omega*. Because this is the Book of Revelation, it seems important that we begin the story of what is to be revealed with the self-revelation of God and God's purpose in the entire sweep of human history. The preacher may wish to focus on the thought that the key to any theology of history is the self-revelation of a God who is creator, redeemer, and will return to renew all things.

Gospel: John 18:33-37. Today's Gospel is one of those vivid and well-known stories which almost preaches itself. The preacher's main task is to channel the wealth of thoughts and images that well forth from the encounter between Jesus and Pilate. John intends to show us the prime example of the encounter between Jesus and earthly power. His vignette offers a striking picture of the pinnacle of earthly success and power in this representative of Roman Empire, meeting the disconcerting figure of Jesus, the monarch of a realm he cannot dream of, much less understand.

The character of Pilate has fascinated people for centuries. John has given him a complex character not matched in the secular records, which present him as a rather insensitive and heavy-handed ruler. But John wants him to personify the power of Rome not just to free Jesus, but to respond to his offer to reveal to Pilate the truth, the key to existence. John presents a Pilate who struggles with his desire to understand the truth of what is happening and be just to Jesus, but at the same time cannot or will not risk exposure to the truth of God that will penetrate and claim his life. Pilate might deign to allow an act of justice to be done, but he will not allow himself to be drawn into Jesus' efforts to lead him into God's life and truth.

To parallel Pilate's motivation with ours can be unnerving and illuminating. Obviously not all congregations are composed of worldly leaders and power brokers, but everyone has faced crucial moments of choice. Will we allow Jesus' light and truth to illumine our lives—in effect, will we accept Jesus' sovereignty in our lives—or will we withdraw and protect ourselves from him and the judgment he occasions in us?

The figure of Jesus is also a compelling focus. What is kingship? Much of the Last Supper, with its discourses and passion account, treats that theme. In John, Jesus' apparently most profound abasement is also his glorification. His appearance before Pilate embodies that key of Johannine theology. To relate that dimension of Jesus' sovereignty to contemporary notions of leadership and power will certainly allow much opportunity for reflection with regard to individual and corporate behavior. A sermon that focuses in depth on one or two situations or examples can be most effective.

Another direction the sermon might take is to look deeply into the dynamics of the encounter between Jesus and Pilate about the character of truth. For Jesus, truth is intimately connected with God's life and our living attuned to God's purposes. It is somewhat unclear what Pilate thinks truth is, but he does not want it (or God) to touch his life. Pilate's refusal to respond to Jesus, and Jesus' own invitation to him can offer a powerful analysis of the process through which we evade or respond to God's claim on our lives.